THE A TO Z OF SOCCER

The A to Z of Soccer

MICHAEL PARKINSON &
WILLIS HALL

With drawings by BOB MONKHOUSE

PELHAM BOOKS

First published in Great Britain by
PELHAM BOOKS LTD
52 *Bedford Square,*
*London, W.C.*1
1970

7207 0383 2

Set and printed in Great Britain by
Tonbridge Printers Ltd, Peach Hall Works, Tonbridge, Kent,
in Baskerville eleven on thirteen point, on paper supplied by
P. F. Bingham Ltd, and bound by James Burn
at Esher, Surrey

CONTENTS

A is for . . .

Association Football

Association Football is the sport to which you have chosen to dedicate your life. Never look back, you have made a wise decision. There are other vocations, equally demanding, which might have taken your fancy. You could have chosen to become a monk in a closed order, or you might have made voluntary application for a lifetime of service on an Arctic weather station. But no, you have decided to give your heart and risk your sanity by supporting a football club – one club, richer or poorer, for better or for worse; for the fight against relegation to the fourth division or the ultimate triumph of the Cup Final at Wembley Stadium. You have made your choice and you will never have cause to regret it, although there may be times when your wife will be none too pleased.

Whether you have spent a score of rain-soaked seasons behind the goal-mouth, or if next Saturday is to be the day on which you take your first long walk to the nearest football ground, this book is intended to be of some assistance and to explain just a few of the enigmas in the greatest game in the world.

Legend tells us that Association Football was invented when a certain gallant, if somewhat impetuous, tribal Briton decapitated a Roman Centurion and then proceeded to celebrate his victory by booting the helmeted head across the playing fields of Londinium. In the excitement of the moment he was joined in sport by several of his fur-clad, spear-carrying friends. Thus was Soccer born. And from that day to this, the art of football has figured largely in the proud heritage of British History.

Sir Francis Drake, for example, and contrary to a folk-lore tale concerning a bowling green, beat three men and slotted

home a copy-book goal for Plymouth Argyle before turning his attentions to the Spanish Armada.

The Tolpuddle Martyrs were a Sunday League village team of swede-bashers who kept losing their ball in the local duck-pond.

Stephenson's Rocket was a goal smashed into the net from forty-five yards in the closing seconds of a Darlington second round F.A. Cup-tie and subsequently had a steam-engine named after it.

The story is often told of the unofficial armistice during the 1914–18 War when a handful of German soldiers met a group of British tommies on Christmas Day in No-Man's Land and enjoyed a scratch game of football. What is not generally known is that the Great War was restarted after a German machine-gunner went over the top of the ball to a Lancashire fusilier's shin and refused to accept the referee's decision.

The great game has progressed and refinements have been added since the days of the Roman Invasion. The Ancient Britons now wear an all-white strip and call themselves England, the Romans put on striped shirts and Adidas boots and are known as Italia, the aid has been enlisted of an old chap with a whistle, the number of participants has been stabilised, the size of the playing area has been regulated – and so it goes on.

But, and never forget the fact, when one player is struck down and a steel-studded boot goes into his teeth that this was the first true intent of the sport, this is what football is all about. Though the rules may alter, the original spirit lives on.

Amateur Football

An amateur footballer is different from a professional footballer. He gets paid less. He is not supposed to get paid at all being one of that select band of unstained sportsmen who play for love and not for pennies; but we all know that to be a very old fashioned idea nowadays. Nonetheless no one in amateur football will ever admit that money is involved. Players and officials alike maintain a tight-lipped silence whenever the question of illegal payments comes up.

The use of the word 'amatcur' is British hypocrisy at its worst. The British are generally more hypocritical than the people of other nations and it shows most of all in their attitude toward sport. The amateur ideal was invented and fostered by the British because it suited their slogan that the game's the thing. In fact as any sensible sportsman knows, the result is the thing that really matters. Amateurs are supposed to be different people to professionals. Amateurs are super chaps with noble profiles and clean limbs who say 'sorry' when they break your leg. Amateurs live up to that marvellous British ideal that sex and sport don't mix. Indeed it is supposed that amateurs take up soccer to keep their minds off the birds and whenever nonetheless they find the urge coming on they take a cold shower. That is the belief. In fact amateur soccer players like their professional brothers are the biggest pullers of birds in the business. Cyclists are too busy eating glucose tablets to bother with women, rugby players are too pre-occupied getting stoned and singing dirty songs to dally long with a maiden and cricketers are

frightened of getting their flannels dirty. But soccer players are one hundred per cent dedicated to giving maximum play to their real instincts. It is often said as a criticism of soccer, both amateur and professional, that unlike other sports there is no social side to the game. What these people don't understand is that supping ale is not the only pleasure of life. Soccer players discovered a long time ago that there is as much fun to be had in the back of a car as in a clubhouse. Furthermore it is cheaper.

Generally speaking the basic differences that exist between the amateur player and his professional brother is that they both play for the same rewards – namely money and crumpet – but the amateur gets less of it. The lesson to be drawn from this by any aspiring soccer player is that if he is greedy he must become a professional but if, like most of us he likes things in moderation and doesn't want to pay income tax, then he should turn amateur.

Animal

An animal is a fourteen stone footballer who is kept chained up for six days a week and let loose for ninety minutes

exercise on Saturday afternoons. An animal is not properly fed but his appetite is whetted occasionally by chunks of red meat slung at him by the team manager. Some animals are quite tame, even friendly, during their week-day captivity but these are the ones most feared when enjoying their exercise period. An animal is made of bone and muscle and is mostly to be found in a defensive position. It is not unusual for a striker to fall back, in total disregard of his manager's instructions, and play a midfield role when he spots an animal in the opposing team. On such occasions the striker is reported to have had a quiet game.

B is for . . .

Banana Ball

The art of delivering a banana ball lies in the ability to bend a ball in flight. A player adept in the skills of the banana kick will prove a useful adjunct to your side.

A banana ball is often attempted from a direct free-kick position. The player, taking the kick, tries to swerve a rising ball past the wall of defenders and dip it into the top corner of the net. If he succeeds, the goal-keeper is left unsighted, helpless and covered in chagrin. You will applaud a successful banana ball when it is executed by a member of your own team but, should your side suffer the humiliation of having a goal scored against them in this manner, you may safely lay the blame on a lucky slice carried into the net by strong prevailing winds.

Best

B is for Best Footballer and Best Looking who just happens to be George Best. He more than any other modern player symbolises the metamorphosis of the footballer from a shabby wage slave with short back and sides to a long-haired pop idol with money in the bank and enough sex appeal to fill a warehouse. George Best is still only a young man in his early twenties but he is already a legend as much for the glamour that surrounds him as for his magnificent skills as a player.

He grew up in Northern Ireland part of a happy but poor family and was kicking a football as soon as he could walk. As a teenager he looked like a stick of undernourished rhubarb and it was his appearance of frailty that counted against him as he was watched by many talent scouts for

English clubs. Fortunately for the soccer public in general and Manchester United in particular, one scout had the good sense to see that what George Best lacked in size he more than compensated for in skill. Working on the principle that you can always put weight on a player but you can't teach genius, the scout persuaded Best to join Manchester United. He was seventeen when he played his first senior game and from the very beginning it was obvious that a new and major star had entered the arena.

It is always difficult to analyse genius, to put a finger on the quality that separates a great player from a good one, and so it is with Best. Suffice it to say that whatever qualities are needed to make a great player he has them all in abundance. His skills are nothing short of phenomenal. He can beat an opponent with every known trick in the book plus a few that he invented himself and moreover, do the whole bag of tricks at top speed. Like all great attacking players he has the ability to accelerate over twenty yards in a manner which makes opponents appear to be nailed to the floor. As a finisher he is deadly with either foot and has the icy precision in a tight situation which is the hallmark of the class marksman. But none of these gifts, formidable though they be, would be of any use to him were he not so courageous. The front runner in modern football has to have guts if he is to do his job properly and a braver player than George Best never put on a pair of football boots. In his very first game at the age of seventeen he suffered the ordeal of being marked by a player not renowned for his love of tricky forwards. The player gave him a going over, a thoroughly professional job, but Best kept coming back for more and in the end, he triumphed. Since then he has had more attention from other people's feet than a hotel door mat but his courage remains unbroken. That is not to say that he has remained totally unchanged. The often brutal treatment he has received has caused him from time to time to lose his cool and do something that he later regretted. In particular he has been known to challenge the referee's decision with disastrous results. All one can hope is as he matures he will learn how to keep his temper in check.

George Best's rise in soccer came at a time when a new and enthusiastic audience for the game was searching for a hero. England had won the World Cup, their success stirred interest in people, particularly women, who previously would not have known a footballer had he bitten them in the leg. What they were looking for was a magician and a glamour-puss and George Best was a natural for the part. He has the looks of a writer of romantic verse, dark curly hair, gentle blue eyes, a sapling body.

He became the first pop idol of soccer. He grew his hair long, often affected a beard or curly moustache and pretty soon every soccer field in Britain had half a dozen youths who looked like him. He became as much a leader and trend setter of his generation as any pop idol or film star. George Best was a very commercial proposition and the world of advertising did not take long to cotton on. He put his name to everything from the virtues of a certain kind of hair dressing to the nutritional value of an egg and by God, how the money rolled in. By the time he was twenty-one, George Best was earning thirty thousand pounds a year and there seemed little to stop him becoming the first man to make a million out of football.

He's older now but the success does not diminish, it just accumulates around his person. The fact is, he grows more successful and more beautiful every day. Whether or not George Best makes a million pounds out of football is more or less beside the point. His importance to the modern game is that he is a landmark. He is a monument in the history of soccer when it became not so much a sport as a part of showbiz.

Boot

B is for boot, and is not to be confused with boots. Boots are the leather articles of footwear, either with moulded rubber soles or steel studs, worn by the players during a match. (See BOOTS) Boot is something which a player puts about, otherwise known as clog, stick, hammer or thump, dependant upon which part of the country you're from.

Boot is the hard man's answer to speed or skills. A ball-juggling fresh-faced front-runner of International class can be whittled down to size by an elderly arthritic full-back who is not averse to putting about a bit of boot. And if it doesn't quite confirm the adage about the tortoise being faster than the hare, at least it proves that the tortoise has a harder skin.

Boot is illegal. Any player caught by the referee in dishing out boot is immediately in line for a caution, or having his name taken, or being dismissed from the field of play. Being dismissed from the field of play carries with it the stigma of an appearance before a disciplinary board where the player

will receive a fine or a suspension, or possibly even both. However, being sent off does carry some slight compensation in that it allows the player the sole use of the communal bath while the water is still hot and clean.

Boots

Boots are used by some to play football in and others to create bovver wiv. It is easy to spot the difference. Soccer boots are smaller and more dainty and are meant for kicking footballs, bovver boots are big and crude-looking and are meant for kicking people. There is an increasing tendency nowadays for footballers to forget the function of soccer boots and use them as one might use bovver boots, namely for kicking someone. (See BOOT). If this attitude persists the police will have no option but to punish soccer players as they do the bovver boys by removing their boots before they get inside the ground.

Bovver

Bovver often happens at a football match. Bovver is caused when two men, alike in every respect except that they support different football teams, meet eyeball to eyeball. At British football grounds bovver is prevented by many policemen and the sensible precaution of putting the fans from team A at the back of one goal and the fans from team B at the back of another goal. This tactic is based on the well known fact that as of the time of writing no one has yet managed to throw a bottle (empty or full) the length of a football pitch. What happens when the fans leave the ground is a matter between them and British Railways.

C is for . . .

Cat

Which is kicked if your team loses. (Also see WIFE BEATING)

Charlton

Bobby Charlton is Britain's best known and most respected player. Charlton's significance in the modern game is not simply due to the fact that he is a great player but more to do with his attitude on the field of play. In an age when many footballers mix the petulance of spoiled brats with the physical approach of dance-hall bouncers, Bobby Charlton is a shining example of controlled professionalism. If he is as much as talked to by a referee it is an event enough to make the headlines. When he is felled by an opponent, as he often is, he allows himself a pitying glance at the offender. Nothing more. When others jostle the referee, questioning his authority, Charlton walks away accepting the decision quietly no matter how ludicrous it might have been. He has the priceless quality of self-control which in the final analysis is that which separates the great sportsmen from those who are simply very good. In an age of whizz kids, swingers and Flash Harrys, there is something very reassuring about Bobby Charlton. He stands for those old-fashioned virtues of good manners and unassuming charm which the post-war generations have supposedly scrapped.

He was one of the famous Busby Babes, conceived and nursed by Busby and destroyed at Munich airport on their way home from a European Cup semi-final. Charlton, like Busby, survived the crash, overcame the horror and became the foundation stone on which Busby built yet another great team. Charlton thinks Busby is the greatest manager in the world, Busby thinks Charlton is the greatest player in the world. Few would argue with either opinion.

When Bobby Charlton was born there was little doubt that he would be a professional footballer. His mother, Cissie, is a member of Britain's most famous footballing family, the Milburns of Ashington, Northumberland. He was a brilliant schoolboy footballer who turned down offers from a dozen top league clubs to join Manchester United on leaving school. He has been there ever since, learning his craft and learning it well enough to become what he is today, a master footballer.

Charlton is a rarity, at one and the same time the architect who designs a game, the artist who adorns it. He is one of that select band of footballers whose deeds are burned on the brain and who can bring a Press box full of journalists (who have seen most things this side of heaven) to their feet in unashamed admiration. He doesn't look a thoroughbred when he steps on to a field. At first glance you'd imagine him being more suited to donkey-work than artistic endeavour. The trunk is sturdy and built for stamina, the legs are fearsome, resembling those normally employed in holding up billiard tables. But in action he is beautiful. There is no other word. On the ball and in full flight he is one of the most noble sights in football, a superb blend of grace and athleticism, a heady mixture of delicacy and power. For a man who can make people's spines tingle, he is remarkably undemonstrative. He gets very pink-faced and Anglo Saxon during the ritual cuddling which follows one of his goals. His modesty is alarming and the despair of sports writers eager for the revealing quote.

Some time ago, after two wonderful displays against Benfica in the European Cup, Charlton received rave write-ups. Bela Guttman, one of the most knowledgeable men in football said that if Benfica had Charlton they would win the World Cup, never mind the European bauble.

Charlton was pressed for his reaction to this praise. Wasn't he thrilled, elated even by what Guttman had said. He thought for a moment and replied, 'People are entitled to their opinion.' In the frenetic world of football Bobby Charlton is a serene figure unaffected by the adoration of his fans, seemingly unruffled by the pressures that place an intolerable load on his shoulders.

Fashions change in footballers. Some stars of one generation are forgotten by the next. Bobby Charlton will remain forever in the minds of those fortunate enough to have seen him. He is that curiously old-fashioned but nonetheless priceless creature: a player and a gentleman.

Chopper

Chopper is the nickname bestowed by fans on the robust, hard-tackling member of their team. Fans of luckless opposing teams are inclined to refer to the same player in less endearing terms. (See ANIMAL)

Cigarette Cards

Cigarette cards are small oblong pieces of cardboard which cigarette manufacturers used to give away with each and every packet of their product. Cigarette cards are often decorated with the head and shoulder likenesses of sun-bronzed, granite-faced footballers with string tying up the necks of their jerseys and their hair parted down the middle.

Cigarette card collecting was the hobby of small boys and pimply youths whose growth had been stunted by an early addiction to nicotine. In the good old days, footballers never collected cigarette pictures of their own images because, in the good old days, athletes shunned tobacco. Nowadays most footballers smoke like chimneys (see COACH), but cigarette manufacturers have stopped manufacturing pictures of athletes. We suspect there is a moral in it.

Close Season

The Close Season happens during those frighteningly long and barren weeks over the summer months when football stops being played. Professional footballers like the Close Season because their clubs tog them out in brand-new blazers with gold-wire crests, snazzy light-weight trousers, Panama straw hats, and send them off on tour. They clamber aboard jet-liners and zoom off to strange-sounding places like Zambia or Bolivia where they play friendly matches against foreigners who are always smaller than themselves. Before these games they exchange club pennants as a gesture of goodwill and peace between nations and then the two teams go out on the pitch and clog each other into the ground. After the match the players go off to small dark friendly bars and chat up small dark friendly ladies and drink vodka and gin and various exotic local brews. They get drunk and swop their Panama hats for sombreros and purchase examples of local craftsmanship from the natives such as Parker pens and Rolex watches. By and large, they enjoy themselves.

Amateur footballers also go on tour during the Close Season but they have to pay for themselves. They go to places like Dublin and Belfast where they consume vast quantities of draught Guinness and are often sick and sometimes never play football at all.

Footballers' wives don't go on tour, they stay at home and look after babies and are glad when the Close Season finishes.

Football supporters don't like the Close Season. They spend their Saturday afternoons accompanying their wives to shopping complexes where they carry armfuls of carrier bags bulging with sprouts and potatoes or, at best, they sit at home and watch Cyclo-cross and wrestling on television and make bets on horses.

Luckily, for football supporters, the Close Season gets shorter every year.

SHADE in SUMMER FOOTBALL

Closet Winger

A closet winger is rare nowadays because you can't get the closets. Once upon a time he dominated world football. He was a British invention, invariably a short man with bandy legs who as a short child with bandy legs learned his technique by flicking the ball against a row of closets (or outside toilets as they will be known south of Rugby) and collecting the rebound. Nowadays this technique applied on the field of play is termed a 'wall pass' and it is typical of the faint hearts that run British soccer that it is not given its proper name. When Britain ruled the soccer world was when every street in every Northern village, town or city boasted a decent row of outside closets. Our decline as a world power commenced when supposedly enlightened town planners started building houses with built-in toilets, yet another example of a retrograde step made in the name of progress.

Closet wingers were not only tricky but very fast off the mark as they had to be when, as often happened, one of their passes burst through the closet door to reveal the occupant who did not take kindly to receiving guests with his trousers round his ankles. The great closet wingers were players like Stanley Matthews, Tom Finney and the little

A NIMBLE MINER DISPROVING THE THEORY THAT MAN WITH TROUSERS DOWN CANNOT CATCH CLOSET WINGER WITH TROUSERS UP.

known Geronimo of Grimethorpe who looked like being the greatest of the lot until his career was nipped in the bud when one of his passes disturbed the early morning ablutions of a large and nimble miner who disproved the theory that man with trousers down cannot catch closet winger with trousers up.

Sir Alf Ramsey gave back a lot of Britain's self-respect when he won the World Cup in 1966 with a team which became known as the wingless wonders. Many soccer theoreticians have praised Ramsey for what they considered to be a considerable piece of tactical super-think. Nothing could be further from the truth. The person who dictated the tactics of that team was the man who invented the inside toilet.

Coach

Every club has two team coaches and it is useful, from the off, to be able to distinguish one from the other. There is the coach who wears a track suit, carries a sponge, and nips smartly on to the pitch (see Diagram A), whenever one of his players is injured. The other team coach is approximately thirty-two feet long (see Diagram B), and belts up and down the motorways at incredible speed. Try not to confuse the two if their names are brought up in conversation.

For instance, if you are told that your team is travelling to its next away fixture on the team coach, you can safely assume that the lads are going to the game in a thirty-two foot bus and not being given a piggy-back by a gentleman with a plastic shoulder-bag. On the other hand, should you read in your classified results newspaper that the team coach was called on to the pitch during a match, this will not mean that a thirty-two foot bus was brought on as substitute. An easy way to tell the two apart is to remember that the thirty-two foot bus is wired for Radio One and Hymns of Praise, whereas the coach in the track suit hurls foul obscenities from his seat on the touch-line.

The coach which is thirty-two foot long seats forty passengers and a driver. When your team is travelling to or from an away game, the manager, the chairman and the board of directors always sit at the front end of the coach where they argue about football and team tactics. While the club officials are having their discussion, the players and the substitute sit at the back of the coach where they play cards for money.

The team coach (the one which is thirty-two foot long) is fitted with forty ash-trays which are never used – it is forbidden to smoke on the team coach because the manager and the club officials believe that it would be bad for their players health to travel up and down the country in a smoke-filled bus. The club officials never smoke on the coach, they suck hardboiled sweets, munch chocolates and fill the ash-trays with toffee papers, but they do not grow fat as they worry a great deal.

The players, who are not in total sympathy with the beliefs of the officials, all smoke like crazy, but as they sit at the back of the bus they are able to blow their smoke and knock their ash out of the windows without the manager or the board of directors seeing them. The players do not suck hard-boiled sweets but they *are* inclined to put on weight as they don't worry about a blind thing. Because they are inclined to grow fat, the playing staff have to report to the club every morning and indulge in hard training. The manager, the chairman and the board of directors never have to train at all.

The team coach who runs on to the pitch with a wet sponge also travels to the away matches in the team coach which is thirty-two foot long, which can be confusing for the other passengers on the bus. In order to simplify matters, if the manager, or one of the club officials, wishes to speak to team coach 'A' on team coach 'B' he will most probably address him by his first name, rather than refer to him as 'coach'. 'Excuse me, John (or Jack, or James, or whatever the coach's name happens to be), but do you happen to have a boiled sweet about your person?' Which is a silly question because it is common knowledge that the coach in the track suit never carries anything about his person except Dextrosol tablets and sticks of chewing gum. But the manager has used the coach's first name, in this instance, in order that the players and the club officials will not imagine that he is addressing a thirty-two foot bus, thus presenting himself in their eyes as a stark, raving lunatic. Off the bus, and in general company, the manager drops this first name familiarity and addresses the team coach as 'coach'. This is because the majority of football supporters already *know* that their team's manager *is* a stark, raving lunatic, so there is no need for him to put up a front.

The team coach in the track suit never refers to himself as 'coach', or by the name his mother gave him. If you should chance to bump into your club's coach at your local grey-

hound stadium (which is the likeliest place to meet him on his day off), he will tell you that his official position is that of club phsyiotherapist. Physiotherapist is a long word which you need not commit to memory as all it means is a man in a track suit who carries a wet sponge.

Corners, Crosses to the Far Post, and Chopping Down an Opposing Player

Chopping down an opposing player is a fair defensive tactic if it is employed by one of your own team's backs when he remains the last bastion of defence between the opposition's centre-forward and your own goal-mouth. Chopping down a player is a disgusting affront to sportsmanship when it is perpetrated by one of the roughneck hooligans on the other side.

Custodian of the Citadel

See GOALKEEPER.

Cricket

The cricket season is the time of year in England when it is too wet to play football.

D is for . . .

Defeat

There are two forms of defeat, deserved and undeserved, and it is difficult to say which of the two is more bitter. An undeserved defeat is one when your team have run their hearts out and their legs off for the whole ninety minutes, when they have done everything possible with the ball except slip it into the back of the net, when they have had ninety-nine-point-nine per cent of the game, when they have diddled rings round the opposition, when the only time that your rivals' forwards have been inside your half it has been to score the only goal. You will find it hard to take. A deserved defeat is one when your lot have stood around the pitch for the whole of the game with about as much idea as a lot of plastic jelly-babies and the opposition's goal tally looks like a cricket score.

In either case, defeat is unbearable.

If you are to last in the rough-tough hurly-burly world of football supporting, a lot will depend on how you learn to take defeat. You must never try to be a good loser, for that way lies insanity. If you walk around the world with a brave face, your head held high, but with all the problems of football failure bubbling about in your mind, it stands to reason that you will be doomed for relegation to a strait-jacket. You will stand about as much chance of survival as the Scilly Isles have got of snatching the World Cup. And besides, it's not your job to maintain a cool head at all times. Your club is paying good money to its manager to do just that thing. No, in defeat your duty is plain:

Go home. Go directly home. Do not speak to anyone, least of all your wife. Throw your dinner at the wall. Go to bed. Stay in bed. Act like a man, take a week off work.

By the time the following Saturday comes around you'll feel a whole lot better for it. When the clarion call of the Public Address System calls you from your bed, summons you to the ground, you'll be fit and willing once again to take up your position on the popular terraces. Then, as the lads run out on the pitch, you will be ready to urge them on with heart and voice and scarf and rattle to certain victory.

Defeat? Good sir, you will not know the meaning of the word.

Defensive Play

Defensive Play is the curse of modern football. Ever since managers discovered that it is easier to prevent the other team scoring goals than to score goals themselves, the modern game has been bedevilled by negative, defensive tactics. Long gone are the days when teams attacked with five forwards spurred on by two attacking wing halves. Nowadays the player allowed to play in his opponent's half has as much contact with his team mates as a leper.

This mania for defence can be seen at most league grounds on a Saturday afternoon when most teams, who would have you believe they are playing 4–2–4 or 4–3–3, are in fact playing 9–0–1. Taken to its logical conclusion, this means that eventually some master-mind will see the sense of playing ten players across the goal line. If he chooses his players according to precise physical measurements he should guarantee being able to block up the goalmouth so that not even a draught can get through. All he has to do then is play one fleet-footed striker who operates in his own penalty area picking up the rebounds from his team mates as the other team plays shots-in. This may sound absurd, but it could happen. When it does will be the time when greyhound racing takes over from soccer as the most popular sport in Britain. (See WEMBLEY STADIUM)

Desperate Tactics

Desperate tactics is a phrase much-loved by football reporters to add a touch of professional journalistic excitement to a very dull report about a very dull game.

For example, the keen sports-newshawk for the *Amersley Weekly Guardian* (a spotty bespectacled eighteen-year-old youth in a green corduroy jacket), covering a no-score match between Amersley Casuals and Worsthorpe Wanderers, might enliven his column to the effect that 'early in the second half Amersley employed desperate tactics and flung everyone up in attack'.

Similarly, the equally bright lad covering the game for the *Worsthorpe and District Clarion* could, after the final whistle, phone his sports desk and relay for the benefit of his news-hungry readers that 'early in the second half Worsthorpe employed desperate tactics and pulled everyone back in defence'.

The true sequence of events may well have been that the

youth from the *Guardian* invited the lad from the *Clarion* to join him for a drink in the supporters' club at half-time and, missing the second half altogether, they drunk each other under the table on ginger-beer shandies.

Dynamic

Dynamic is an adjective which pleases footballers when it is used to describe them.

E is for . . .

Easy-Easy!

Easy-easy! is a taunt that may be levelled against your team (and therefore indirectly at yourself), by the uncouth ill-mannered rabble of supporters who are cheering on the other side. *Easy-easy*! is a pill made all the more bitter to swallow by the fact that it is usually proferred at a time when your unfortunate lads are two or more goals in the red.

There is little that you can do to counter the accusation *Easy-easy*! Firstly, if your side is a handful of goals in arrears, you will hardly be in a mood for apt witticisms and, secondly, if you can take anything like an unbiased view of the situation, you will be forced to admit that there must be some slight grain of truth in the taunt.

However, there are a couple of possible get-outs which you might hold up your sleeve. It is conceivable that your team is a notch higher up the league table than your opponents. In which circumstance your rallying cry across the terraces to the opposing supporters will be: OH, OH, OH-OH-OH-OH! WE'RE GONNA BEAT YOU IN THE LEAGUE! Or, again, it is possible that your heroes are still in the glory of the fight for the F.A. Cup, while the load of old rubbish, who are having the run of the ball plus all the luck on the afternoon in question, were dislodged from the road to Wembley weeks ago. If this be the case, try: OH, OH, OH-OH-OH-OH! WE'RE GONNA WIN THE F.A. CUP!

Either or both of the above retaliatory chants are worth a shot, although it must be admitted that neither come across with any force or real sense of purpose. No, if you are more than two goals down it is more than enough. Hold your peace and face up to facts. Suffer the fools gladly. Allow the fat-headed twits on the opposing terraces their ill-fated moment of glory. Let them bawl their stupid heads off like a lot of hysterical parrots. Bide your time. Wait until next season for the identical fixture – it might well be your turn then to shout: *Ea*sy-*ea*sy!

Emotional Involvement

No game involves the emotions more than soccer. People might fall in love with cricket, or adore rugby but the man who follows soccer is addicted to the game. It can become the all-consuming passion of his life whereby home, family and friends are runners-up in his order of priorities. It can make men ridiculous, persuade them to do crazy things. It transforms sober-suited office workers into multi-coloured, raucous fanatics; it makes street fighters out of men who normally would never say Boo to a goose. It leads some men to drink and others to leave their wives. A man who would never contemplate holidaying abroad because he doesn't like wogs, the food is greasy and they don't speak English, will nonetheless throw away a lifetime's prejudice to see his team play anywhere in the world. He will follow them to the furthest ends of the earth without concern for his pocket or the prospect of gyppy-tummy.

The excesses of emotional involvement in soccer are incredible but true. There is the Liverpool fan who calls his house 'The Kop', has it decorated in red and white and who gave his son the christian names of Ian St. John. There are many brides who have spent their honeymoon at Arsenal Stadium and their first night being told how Charlie George scored the winning goal, and there is one recorded case of a fan who cared so much about his team that he hurled a hand-grenade at the opposing goalkeeper just to let him know how he felt. The hand-grenade was a dud, but the goalkeeper wasn't to know that.

There is little doubt that the fans who become most

emotionally involved with a soccer team come from the north of Britain and Glasgow in particular. The point was made when twenty-five thousand Celtic fans went all the way to Milan to see their team in the final of the European Cup. Their addiction to the game led some of them into curious adventures. For instance, there was the man who arrived back at Glasgow on an aeroplane only to remember as he went through customs that he had driven to Italy in his motor car. But the most revealing story of the lot concerned the party that chartered an aeroplane and on the return journey had a whip round and presented the startled captain with twelve pounds ten and sixpence in silver as a token of their appreciation. It was no use telling them that what is standard practice on coach outings does not apply to charter aircraft because they were in the grip of football fever, a disease for which there is no known cure.

F is for . . .

Fantasy

Every man or child who ever fell in love with soccer knows the value of fantasy. It transports him to the unreal world of pleasant dreams where he, the night shift worker from Dagenham becomes Dead-Eyed Dick the most feared marksman in the football league. In his first season with Manchester United he scores in every game, nets a hat trick at Wembley, puts four past Brazil in Rio, opens a night club in Salford and marries Princess Anne. Fantasy is harmless if it is kept private, a matter between the individual and his mind. When it becomes public it is pathetic and even tragic. There is for instance the recorded case of the supporter who turned up at every game wearing his team's full strip underneath his street clothes. Thus attired and carrying his boots in a paper bag under his arm, he would stand behind the goals at every game, waiting for the day when someone was injured and the announcement came over the loudspeaker: 'Will anyone who has brought his boots to the game report to the manager's office immediately as we are a man short.'

In the perfect fantasy this state of affairs would occur in the last period of extra time in the semi-final of the F.A. Cup and our hero would take the field and score the winning goal in the dying seconds. He would then be chaired from the field and offered a ten year contract worth a hundred thousand quid which he would refuse while everyone looked on with open-mouthed amazement. He would then slip out of the ground unnoticed and return to his council house in Dagenham while the press and television hunted for the mystery soccer genius who came out of the terraces and won a semi-final. That, of course, would be the perfect fantasy.

What really happened was that the announcement never came and the supporter simply suffered a lifetime behind the goal as the most overdressed spectator in the land. Even that would have been bearable had it not been for an unfortunate event which exposed his fantasy to public ridicule. During one game, and due no doubt to the fact that he was wearing twice as many clothes as anyone else, the supporter fainted. He was taken away by ambulance men who removed his top layer of clothing to investigate the damage and underneath his waistcoat found his guilty secret. Word got around, the story was picked up by the Press and one man's private fantasy became the object of public scrutiny and ridicule. In future, whenever he attended a game and a player became injured he would be urged by the spectators to take the field and do his stuff. Finally, unable to endure it any longer, he abandoned soccer and took up pigeon racing. That sad and true story is a caution to everyone who ever dreamed of being Bobby Charlton. The secret is to keep it to yourself because one man's fantasy is another man's belly laugh.

FIFA

The world soccer organisation and symbol of the brotherhood, fellowship and goodwill spread throughout the world by the game of soccer. (See also WORLD CUP and WAR)

Footballers' Wives

Footballers' girl-friends, when they become footballers' wives, soon discover that they've drawn the short straw in the marriage-to-a-celebrity stakes. They are accorded treatment that doesn't match up with the mode of living of the helpmates of the famous in other fields.

A film-star's wife will accompany him across continents

when he makes a movie – a footballer's wife sits at home holding the baby while her husband is on tour. A politician's wife influences her husband's career by her choice of guests and menus at elaborate dinner parties – a footballer tends to keep his home life to himself and only on rare occasions invites a friend round for the odd cup of cocoa. The wife of an actor starring in the West End will hold her spouse's hand in the dressing room until the very minute before he goes on stage – no footballer's wife has even so much as seen inside the room where her hubby puts on his football togs. A footballer's wife is a sparrow in an eagle's nest, a country mouse keeping home for a town lion. Footballers' wives seldom complain.

Footballers' wives are, of necessity, a gregarious bunch who stick together because football clubs tend to mistrust them. The presence of footballers' wives at football matches is suffered rather than welcomed – some poor lasses are even barred from attending games on the grounds that they possess the evil eye. The ones that do get to see their husbands in action are not allowed in the dressing rooms, the board rooms, or any of the offices, neither are they invited to take tea with the directors' ladies at half-time. As a half-hearted attempt by the clubs to show that they are aware of the girls' existence, the players' wives are usually allotted a small room to themselves (known as the Ladies' Room), where they are served with cups of tea, quite often without benefit of saucers. They are also grudgingly offered a plate of fish-paste sandwiches and a stack of sausage rolls which have been cut in half in order to make them go round.

During the ninety minutes playing time the footballers' wives are not invited into the directors' box; they are given seats among the paying customers where they sit together proudly watching their hubbies gad about the pitch and, like a collection of over-zealous nannies in Hyde Park, complain bitterly when their loved ones are upended by their bullying playmates.

Match-days apart, footballers' wives are rarely in the public eye, except on the sports page of their local paper when they have just given birth – or on the front page of a Sunday newspaper if they are clever enough to go through labour on a Saturday afternoon while their husband is actually on the field of play.

Footballers' wives do have their moments of glory. When footballing husbands go into the transfer market their wives are flattered and wooed by prospective managers with a plethora of domestic promises: fitted carpets, central heating, front and back gardens, high speed gas, close access to a nursery school and the firm promise of a tip-up seat at Wembley in close proximity to Her Majesty the Queen, provided the club should have the good fortune to reach the final of the F.A. Cup.

And on Cup-Final day twenty-two lucky wives and fiancées come into their own. Footballers' wives are not, generally speaking, fast followers of the vagaries of fashion (give them a twin-set, a string of cultured pearls and a sheepskin lined coat for the January fixtures and they are happy enough for the most part), but on Cup-Final day anything goes. Anything from a Carnaby Street rig-out purchased after three sherries the evening before, to a bouffant hair-do dyed in the club's colours. Footballers' wives are a loyal lot. Footballers' wives are nice.

Free Transfer

A free transfer is what clubs give to a player when they have no further use for him and furthermore know that no other club would touch him with a long barge pole. A free transfer is the player's passport to the knacker's yard. Some players have survived a free transfer and made a name for themselves but in the main a free transfer on a player means he starts seeking further employment in another occupation.

G is for . . .

Ghost Writer

A Ghost Writer is a man who writes something and then lets someone else put his name to it. He performs this service for soccer players who not unnaturally do not baulk at the idea of being paid for the privilege of letting someone else do the donkey-work. Ghosted articles and books are on the whole very forgettable and add nothing to the knowledge of what really goes on inside a footballer's skull. The books tend to have short, dramatic titles such as *Flashing Boots* or *Cannonball Kid* and always start in the same way. Thus: 'I was born only a corner-kick away from Highbury Stadium (or White Hart Lane, Maine Road, Hillsborough, Villa Park, Old Trafford, Molyneux, Stamford Bridge, etc., etc.)'. Then there is always a chapter about: 'The Day I Broke Down and Wept', another about 'My World Eleven', and yet another entitled 'I owe it all to Tommy Docherty (Matt Busby, Joe Mercer, Brian Clough, Don Revie, Alec Stock, Stan Cullis, Tony Waddington, etc., etc.)'.

It is remarkably easy to ghost a book. All the writer does is find a quiet corner, set a tape recorder working and let the player speak. Then he turns it into reasonable English and awaits the letter telling him he has won the Nobel Prize for Literature. Ghosting a match report is an altogether more difficult business. It calls for some of the disciplines of journalism, such as writing to length in a suitable style, twin necessities that are meaningless to most soccer players. Therefore this imaginary scene in a press box is not as far-fetched as it might seem:

Ghost: 'That was a great goal. What shall I say happened?'

Ex-player: 'Well, Charlie banged it down the middle like and Joe knocked it in.'

Ghost: 'Would I be right in saying then that you would describe that goal as follows: "Getting the ball in his own half, Jones sped down the wing and beat three men in a scintillating burst. His centre from the right was pinpointed for Smith who rose out of a ruck of players, seemed to hang for a moment in mid-air and then powered a header into the corner of the net. The goalkeeper stood immobile as the ball whizzed past him, a mute and helpless spectator to Smith's brilliance."?'

Ex-player: 'Yuh, that's right. Couldn't have said it better meself.'

The opposite problem to this is posed by the player who has passed an F.A. coaching course and sees patterns of play that the poor ghost writer never imagined existed. This is what happens then:

Ghost: 'That was a bad miss by Smith.'

Ex-player: 'Not really. You see, he was acting as decoy in that move taking the defence out of position and creating space at the far post for Roberts. The winger was to blame there because instead of assessing Smith's run correctly and floating the ball to the far post, he played it to the near post where Smith was already tightly marked. Add to that the fact that I happen to know that Smith has an ingrowing toe-nail, his wife left him yesterday and the sun was in his eyes and I reckon we can call that a noble effort.'

Ghost (nods in stunned fashion and writes in book): 'Just before half-time, Smith missed a sitter.' (He makes a mental note to either take an F.A. coaching course or resign his job.)

At present ghost writing is a necessary evil. It might be that sometime in the future as educational standards rise and clubs start recruiting from the universities that there will develop a breed of players capable of writing their own stories. In the meantime any young player would be well advised to spend some of his fortune on a correspondence course in journalism, thus paving the way for the day when the journalist can be freed from the impossible task of putting words into someone else's mouth.

Giant Killers

Every season, and without exception, a humble team from a non-league club or an amateur side filters through, from the Qualifying Rounds of the Football Association Cup, to take on and defeat a League club from the Third or Fourth Division. Such a club is snatched up by the sensation-seekers of the popular press, adulated, lionized, and given the honorary title of giant-killers. This is a title which they hold until the next round of the Cup when, without exception, they are hammered mercilessly into the turf by their new opponents; after which they return to the humble surroundings from which they came and are never heard of again. The giant-killers of football, unlike their counterparts in fairy stories, do not live happily ever after and never ever dispose of more than one giant.

Goalkeeper

Sometimes known as twerp, eejit, or cretino depending which country he is playing in. Goalkeepers are different from other footballers . . . they have less sense. To be a goalkeeper one must be barmy, to be a good goalkeeper one has to be stone crazy. Most goalkeepers are eccentric and it is not yet known whether they were born that way or whether the job made them adopt peculiar ways. One English goalkeeper called Iremonger delighted in taking his team's penalties. In one game he ran the length of the field to take a spot kick, struck the crossbar with a thunderous shot and while galloping back upfield to clear the rebound volleyed a spectacular own goal. Another great goalkeeping eccentric was Chick Farr who played for Bradford Park Avenue. His speciality was pulling down the crossbar when he couldn't be bothered to save a high shot. When admonished by the referee he would pretend to be a foreigner who didn't speak English. Apart from not being normal, a good

goalkeeper must also have the guts of a lion, the constitution of a rhinoceros, the swooping grace of a hawk. It also helps if he is deaf, because no matter how diligently he goes about his task and no matter how brilliantly he performs he will always be first to get a verbal bashing from the fans.

Goalkeepers' mistakes always look worse than any other players' errors and are criticised accordingly. Centre-halves can miskick, centre-forwards can miss open goals and their sins are soon forgotten. But a goalkeeper has only to make one mistake and he is accused of everything from being in the pay of the opposition to becoming blind because of some lewd practice which is supposed to affect the eyesight.

Our advice to any father who catches his son playing at goalkeepers is to nip it in the bud there and then. If allowed to develop it could have serious and lasting consequences.

Groundsman

Of necessity, almost every professional football ground is set in the heart of an industrial town. Football clubs need to be near people. An aerial view of a football ground presents a few acres of carefully nurtured turf surrounded by back-to-back houses; a pleasing landscape in a frame of smoking chimneys. The gentleman responsible for tending the hallowed patch of green is called a groundsman.

A groundsman is a lover of nature and a countryman at heart. A groundsman enjoys his work. For five days of every week, fifty-two weeks of the year, the groundsman is out at daybreak with cutter and trimmer and roller and rake, tending and cultivating, snipping and levelling, doing his utmost to ensure that his pitch is the pride and equal of any other in the Football League. The groundsman knows and loves every square inch of his precious plot.

Every Saturday afternoon, twenty-two young bulls in boots run out on to the pitch and scuff and scar and mutilate the groundsman's handiwork with long, steel studs. Groundsmen, as a general rule, are morose and moody chaps who dislike footballers.

H is for . . .

Half-Time

Half-time happens after forty-five minutes of playing time, plus any extra minutes allowed by the referee for time taken up during the game looking for lost balls or by players fastening their boot-laces. Half-time is a rest period for all concerned with the exception of the people who have paid to come in. For the spectators, half-time is the busiest part of the afternoon, and quite often the most interesting. During half-time the raffle is drawn, other half-time scores are announced, small boys invade the pitch with plastic footballs, scuffles break out, people make new friends, and quite a number of enthusiasts are ejected from the ground by policemen. Sometimes there is even a band.

While all this exciting stuff is going on, the two teams, the referee, the linesmen, the chairman of the club, the board of directors and their wives and ladies, repair to their respective offices and changing rooms where they are all served with a cup of tea – and in the case of the directors and their wives and ladies, a dainty triangular sandwich or an Osborne biscuit.

Half-time takes ten minutes, except in the case of Sunday Football when the allotted time-span is a hundred and twenty seconds during which the players, the referee and the linesman, do not leave the pitch but hang about on the touch-line looking expectantly around in the vague hope that one of the spectators will give them a piece of his orange.

Home Game

A home game is one that is fought out on your own ground – otherwise known familiarly as the patch, the park, the green, or your own midden. Foster your natural pride in your home ground. When you have paid a couple of visits to away matches you will come to realise that your own club has more to offer than any other club on earth.

The turf on your own ground is a lush sward on which every blade of grass is of equal length and weeds are unknown. Your home pitch would do credit to the Head Gardener at Kew. The ball will come off the surface of your own ground with geometrical precision, enabling your own players to judge their passes with computer-like accuracy. You will suffer a small pang of anxiety whenever an alien player kicks up a divot of your home ground turf.

The stands and offices at your home ground exude good-neighbourliness, coupled with the spirit of friendly competitive football. The officials at your ground, from the chairman of the board of directors down to the hot-dog seller outside the terrace gates, are your slaves. The motherly ladies behind the half-time tea-urns at your home ground are ministering angels. You are never short-changed.

Briefly, you will fall pottily in love with your home ground. Try not to let the affair get out of hand, or you will find yourself drawn towards the club, as if by a magnet, even on the days when there is no game being played. You may even stroll round on the odd Thursday evening, just to take a look at the place from the outside, and to satisfy yourself that the main stand has not been damaged by a lunatic pyromaniac since the previous Saturday's game.

Away grounds, you will come to realise, are the total opposite. Away pitches are either nettle-beds or cruel tracts of earth and rock, as uneven and unfriendly as the surface of the moon. Your own team will never find away pitches to their liking, expert ball-players to a man they will founder and falter as their perfectly executed passes go wildly astray on hummocks and mole-hills.

The fellow-fans you mingle with on your own terraces are a chummy lot, lovers of good football to a man, and provided they are treated to a display of football finesse they don't care whether they see their team win or lose – the game is all. They will applaud and encourage a bit of good football from either side and will accord tribute, when deserved, to any player irrespective of the colour of his shirt. Your home fans are an unbiased bunch of good-natured chaps, and you will profit from their example.

The home supporters at away matches are the complete opposite. They wouldn't recognise good football if it was served up to them on buttered toast. They go to see only their own team and are one-sided to the point of insanity. For instance, if one of your defenders should chance to be standing within a mile of their pansy striker as he falls over his own feet in your penalty area, the home fans will hiss, scream and boo, unfairly influencing the referee's decision. If the same thing were to happen at the other end of the pitch, if your centre-forward was tripped, kicked and trodden on by some hooligan, the referee will not pay a blind bit of notice to your quite legitimate protestations.

SUPPORTER and (THWUNK!) SON

Home games, generally, are a joy to watch and are played out before a sporting crowd who know and understand the game they love. Away matches are rough-and-tumbles – free-for-alls enacted in an atmosphere of hatred, ignorance and bigotry.

Hospital Pass

Which is given by Player A to Player B when Player A believes that Player B has been sleeping with his (Player A's) wife. To be technical it is a pass which gives your opponent a better chance of breaking your leg than you have of breaking his.

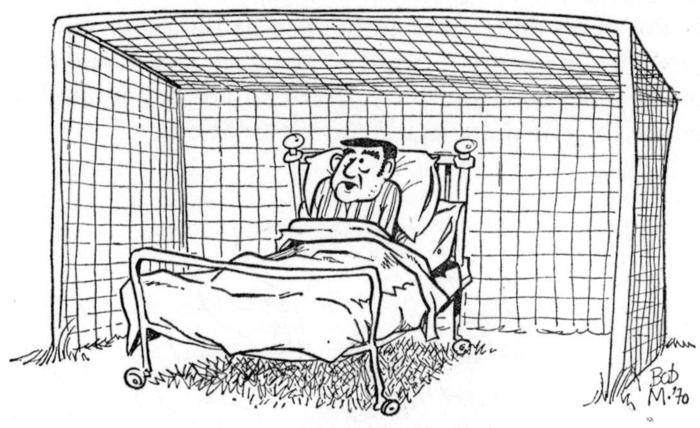

"BED PAN!"

I is for . . .

Inducement

An inducement is an illegal offer made to a player in order to stimulate his game, sharpen his competitive instincts and pull just that little bit more out of him on the field of play. An inducement may take the form of a back-handed fistful of fivers or, in the case of an amateur footballer, threepence-a-mile petrol money and first crack at the manager's wife after the match. Many amateur footballers will be quick to point out that their particular manager's wife cannot be considered an inducement.

Injury Time

Injury time is made up of those urgent, vital seconds added on at the end of a game by the referee to cover time lost by stoppage of play. The amount of time allotted is dependent upon the goal situation after ninety minutes of football. If the opposing team are a goal in arrears then injury time may consist of anything from thirty seconds until however long it takes them to bang the ball in the back of the net. On the other hand, if your lot are a goal down then no injury time is allowable and the referee will blow for full time with the alacrity of a British Imperialist publican on St Patrick's night.

Intellectual

An intellectual is someone who thinks that Georgie Best is the best soloist since Rubinstein. Once upon a time only the lumpen proletariat watched football, it was essentially a working class sport. Today, for reasons that are somewhat obscure, it has been adopted by the upper middle class and the intelligentsia. At any ground you will see a fair sprinkling of high foreheads among the cloth caps. This new audience has demanded and received a new kind of soccer writer. Where once the only requirement of reporting soccer was that the journalist knew which team was which and was a dab hand at alliteration ('Super, sizzling Spurs socked Southampton sideways on Saturday'), today's successful sports writer is in a different class. He is as much at home with the *Oxford Dictionary of Quotations* as the *Football Association Rule Book*. Wherever possible he will use an Italian word like 'Catenaccio' to impress his bank manager and confuse the players he is writing about. His prose style is rotund and full of imagery, thus: 'Jones' run down the wing was a thing of joy, a melody by Strauss, a fusion of the athletic and the spiritual, a lighted taper which touched off the fuse toward the United goal. His shot at goal was savage and unexpected, a streak of summer lightning, a thunderbolt from a blue sky which bulged the net reminding one irresistibly of an Elizabethan's cod-piece.'

Given a lead like this it is not surprising that some of the remarks heard on the terraces nowadays are the sophisticated utterances of men of letters rather than the cruderies of the working class. One example from the terraces of a Third Division club will explain. Two brothers played for this particular club, one talented, one far from talented. It was suspected by the home fans that the not so talented player gained his place because of his brother's influence in the club. This suspicion was given voice during one game when the home team was awarded a penalty and the kick was entrusted to the not so talented brother. His shot from the spot went high over the bar and out of the ground. The crowd was silent for a moment in shock and disbelief and then a voice from the terraces was heard: 'Nepotism. That's what it is, bloody nepotism,' it cried. The anguish of one of soccer's new spectators.

J is for . . .

Jammy Goal

A jammy goal is one which has been scored by the other side.

Jock Stein

Jock Stein is the highly successful manager of a highly successful Scottish football club. (See JOCK STRAP)

Jock Strap

Jock Strap is an article of protective clothing worn by footballers. English soccer fans should try not to confuse the name of this garment with the name of a highly successful manager of a highly successful Scottish football club, particularly if they happen to be in the Hampden Park area. (See JOCK STEIN)

Jokes

There are a lot of jokes about football, most of them born out of despair. A favourite butt of soccer jokes are unsuccessful managers and unsuccessful teams:

'Did you go to see the Rovers last week?'

'No, they didn't come to see me when I was bad.'

Or there's the one about the football fan who rang up his club and found himself speaking to the manager:

Football fan: 'There's a car load of us coming to tonight's match. What time is the kick-off?'

Manager: 'Did you say a car-load?'

Football fan: 'Yes.'

Manager: 'Well in that case, what time would you *like* us to kick off?'

And then there's the one about the unsuccessful manager who went to seek advice from a friend about how he might improve his team's performance. The friend told him to put eleven dustbins on the pitch and let the team dribble in and out of them, recommending this as a successful training tactic. The manager gave the idea a try and the next night rang his friend:

Manager: 'That scheme was no good.'

Friend: 'Why not?'

Manager: 'The dustbins won.'

Goalkeepers are another favourite foil for football raconteurs. There's the joke about the goalkeeper who let in ten goals in one match. After the game, dejected, he trudged into the dressing-room, sat down on the bench and went to put his head in his hands – and missed it. Or there's the one about the goalkeeper whose eyesight was so bad he not only couldn't stop goals being scored; he couldn't find the ball when it was in the back of the net. The same short-sighted goalkeeper, it is said, kicked his cap out three times during one match.

Perhaps the definitive football joke of all time is the one about the Yorkshire fan who, after a life-time of supporting his local team was rewarded with the prospect of a visit to Wembley, his favourites having fought their way into the final of the F.A. Cup. The fan managed to acquire a ticket for the game, journeyed down to London and joined the hundred thousand other lucky souls in England's finest stadium.

Fifteen minutes to kick-off and our fan was overawed by the occasion: flags, rattles, banners, scarves, and Keep Right On To The End Of The Road. Everything was wonderful. It was all as he had imagined it would be – save for one thing. The seat next to his was empty. The following conversation is reported to have taken place between the Yorkshire fan and the middle-aged occupant of the seat beyond the empty one:

Yorkshire fan: 'I can't credit this! It's unbelievable! An empty seat – at Wembley – on Cup Final day!'

Middle-aged Man: 'I can explain that. As a matter of fact, that seat was reserved for my wife. Unhappily, she had the great misfortune to drop down dead last Tuesday.'

Yorkshire fan: 'I'm sorry I spoke, lad. You have my deepest sympathy. But even so, surely you could have given the ticket away? There must be somebody in the family who could have found a use for it?'

Middle-aged Man: 'Family! Family! Don't talk to me about my bloody family! There's not a sportsman among the lot! Every single one of them has gone to the funeral!'

Bred out of remorse and despair, soccer jokes belong to the Theatre of Cruelty but they are a necessary sop to long-suffering fans.

K is for . . .

Kick and Rush

Kick and Rush is an attacking style involving a long, high ball to the heart of the opponent's defence pursued by a centre-forward willing to run through a brick wall. Often used in a derogatory way to denote a lack of sophistication in a team and yet is still a fundamental part of modern soccer.

Known nowadays by its Italian name Cickanrushio.

Kick Anything That Moves

Kick Anything That Moves is a defensive style developed in the early days of soccer by the hard men of north country teams and now much favoured by teams from any part of the world. Its beauty is its simplicity (any fool can do it), and its effectiveness in that if the player on the receiving end is kicked by an expert in the first minute he is not likely to want to play for the other eighty-nine. The utter simplicity of this tactic is summed up in the old saying: 'There are more ways of winning a game than playing football.' Often referred to by its Italian name, Cloggatio.

Kidology

Kidology is much practised on referees by forwards with a talent for acting. The experts in kidology can be tackled thirty yards from goal and yet fall down on the penalty spot. Moreover they can give every impression of having been knocked down by the Flying Scotsman and suffering terrible injuries such as may prove terminal only to rise beaming and without a scratch the moment the referee has given a penalty and sent some poor innocent for an early bath. Some soccer players have given such superb performance of dramatic acting that the Academy of Motion Picture Arts and Sciences might well be moved to include a new category in the Oscar nominations.

L is for . . .

League

Every football supporter firmly believes, at least in his more optimistic moments, that his team is the finest in the land. The League Tables exist to prove him wrong. The sad truth is that there can only be *one* best team and, to forego futile argument, it sits indisputably at the top of the First Division; and until another set of Titans steps in and tumbles the champions from their perch there can be no other claimant to the title.

If you were to ask the man-in-the-street how many leagues there are he would reel off the Four Divisions of the Football League plus, for good measure, the Two Divisions north of the border which are there, he will tell you, solely to make up the numbers on the football coupons. And for him, as far as leagues are concerned, that is about his lot. He couldn't be more wrong. If a complete list of leagues was set down on one long piece of paper it would stretch from Wembley Stadium to a corner flag in a meadow behind the back of a Boy Scout hut somewhere in the East Midlands. For there are more leagues in British football than there are stars in the sky or grains of sand along the seashore.

The professional clubs are followed by the semi-pros, in the wake of the semi-pros come the amateur leagues with strange-sounding titles such as the Isthmian and the Athenian and the Spartan, trailing behind these worthies is a whole world of lesser mortals whose deeds are listed only in the very smallest type in the Sunday newspapers. You may not have heard of them, but they are there. They do battle every Saturday. They win, they lose, they draw and occasionally their matches are abandoned. They have dimensions, senses, affections and passions. If they are kicked they bleed, if they are wronged they retaliate – if they retaliate they are sent off the field.

The First Division teams are the giants of English Football, the successes and failures of the Second, Third and Fourth Division teams are broadcast throughout the land. The achievements of the semi-pros and the amateur lads, struggling in the lowly leagues of football, are seldom publicised, but two hard-fought points won away from home is also life or death to them. (See GIANT-KILLERS)

M is for . . .

Manager

Managers of football clubs come in all shapes and sizes and share the same worried look. Managing a football team is one of the most hazardous occupations in the world. Since the war nearly seven hundred managers have been sacked from British clubs alone and if you laid them end to end you'd have nearly a mile of long-suffering, misery-faced humanity. It doesn't bear thinking about.

Managers are often ex-players who have seen *their* managers suffer and expire and that they should want to follow in their footsteps gives new meaning to the condition known as football daft. Managing a football team is an impossible job because it means trying to talk sense to three largely uncomprehending groups of people essential to any soccer club. Namely: the directors, the players and the crowd. The problem of talking sense to some players is obvious in the definition of soccer as being a simple game played on the whole by the simple-minded for the simple-minded. What good is it explaining Catenaccio to a player who thinks that Naples is at the end of the M1, how frustrating it must be to ask a player 'what is 4–2–4?' and be told in reply, 'ten'. With patience and kindness and tact some managers do uplift their players so that on the field of play they do the job required of them no matter how sophisticated and complex. It is a little more difficult with directors. Directors are kindly, well meaning men who have made a bit of money from their businesses and feel they would like to dabble in the affairs of a football club. If they have any sense they will put their hands in their pockets when asked and leave the running of the team to the manager. Unfortunately most directors believe that they know far more about soccer than most managers and that is why seven hundred managers have been sacked since the war.

This situation of a professional manager being assessed by a bunch of amateurs is unique to soccer. It is like the captain of a jumbo jet being asked to work under the Stoke Poges branch of the British Kite Flying Association. In effect the directors are the tools of the people who pay through the turnstile. All soccer fans think they know more about football than any soccer manager and certainly more than any club director. So when things go wrong for their team they hurl abuse at the board who in turn sack the manager.

You could call it mob rule or you could call it the purest form of democracy practised in the British Isles. It all depends where you are standing when they lower the boom. A manager must never allow himself to take notice of the mob. He can only retain his sanity by turning a deaf ear to them whether they be calling him 'the greatest' for winning the F.A. Cup or next season damning him for a fool because his team were knocked out by Wigan Athletic in the third round.

Fans tell sour jokes about managers. (See JOKES) One concerns the manager who thought he would cheer his team up by buying them a radio for the dressing-room. He was walking toward the ground carrying his purchase under his arm when he was stopped by a fan. 'What's that then?' asked the fan, indicating the radio. 'I've got it for the players,' said the manager, proudly. 'You've done well. It was a good swop,' said the fan, and continued on his way.

The managers who can surmount this kind of pressure and still emerge intact are very special people. They achieve distinction in this most difficult and arduous of professions in different ways. Some, fondly referred to nowadays as 'the track suited managers' achieve success by personal example. They train, play and swear as hard as the man they are employing. It is said of some that they even go to the extremes of denying themselves the company of their wives on the night before a big game. This however must be counted as rumour until someone is brave enough to ask the people concerned.

Others achieve eminence by a single-minded and purposeful dedication to the game of soccer to the exclusion of all else. The most famous example of this latter condition is Bill Shankly, manager of Liverpool. Shankly is immersed in football, his loyalty to the game is complete. There was a story going the rounds that on his wife's birthday Shankly took her to see Barrow Reserves play Accrington Stanley Reserves as a special treat. One day a journalist asked him: 'Tell me Bill, is it true that you took your wife to see Barrow Reserves play Accrington Stanley Reserves as her birthday treat?' Shankly glowered at the journalist and then said: 'There's not a word of truth in it. It was our wedding anniversary.' Other managers, unable to sustain Shankly's unquenchable passion for the game, survive because of their own wit and humour. Joe Mercer of Manchester City is the best representative of this category of manager. Once, before he came to Manchester, when he was managing a club in danger of relegation, he was taken seriously ill. He was visited in bed by the club doctor who was fully aware of the killing pressures on a soccer manager. After he had finished his inspection, Joe brought up the question of paying for the treatment. 'Will you take a cheque?' asked Joe. The doctor looked at Joe in a sorrowful manner. 'Cash if you don't mind, Joe,' he said. 'What a bloody prognosis,' says Joe, re-telling the story with relish.

Why soccer managers, in full possession of the facts of their job, still confess a love for it remains one of the great human mysteries, like the function of the human appendix. In the final analysis a manager's career is a sum total of toilet rolls and laurel wreaths. If at the end of the day he has an equal number of both he will count himself well pleased.

Moore, Bobby

M is for Bobby Moore. If he didn't exist someone would have to invent him. He is everyone's idea of what the perfect athlete should look like even including the noble profile, the blonde hair and the steady blue eyes. He also just happens to be one of the most consistent performers in the game.

The modern game of 4–3–3 or 4–2–4 was made for Bobby Moore who is at his best as a defensive player moving laterally as a sweeper behind his defence. His reading of a game is uncanny and his ability to anticipate a pass and intercept before it reaches its mark more than compensates for his one flaw which is a lack of pace. He is often accused of lacking imagination in his distribution but no one who has seen him adventuring would doubt that he can be as subtle in attack as he is uncompromising in defence.

Moore's greatest asset is his temperament. He brings to every game a poise and self-control which makes him the ideal captain of both his club and his country. He is the sort of player that managers dream of and Sir Alf Ramsey, not renowned for his outbursts of excessive praise, is unequivocal in his praise of Moore. He once said that he regarded Moore as the 'representative' on the field of play and added that he could not imagine a better one. Off the field Moore is a pleasant young man, but cautious in his relations with all but his closest friends. He dresses like a male model, runs a couple of successful businesses and is married to a ravishing girl called Tina. Bobby Moore has everything but it's all well under control. He rarely makes headlines like George Best, he's not noisy. Quietly and without fuss he goes on, year in year out, being a very good professional footballer who just happens to look like a Greek God.

Mutual Consent

You may read in the sporting pages of your favourite newspaper that a football club manager has withdrawn his services by the mutual consent of himself and the Board of Directors. You may pause to wonder what is meant by a statement such as this.

What happens is that the manager (let us call him Mr E.) is invited to attend before the board one morning after training. In all probability he trots round to the boardroom hotfoot in a sweaty track suit, the prospect of a raise in salary at the back of his mind. No such luck.

'Mr E., you're sacked,' says the Chairman.

'Fair enough,' comes back the luckless Mr E.

And a decision of club policy arrived at in this manner is known, in footballing circles, as being by mutual consent. The despondent Mr E. leaves the boardroom, mooches back to his private office, packs his personal belongings and ponders upon what Santa Claus will bring for his little ones on Christmas morning. In the harsh world of football club managership, the consent is usually more mutual on the directors' side.

N is for . . .

Nancy, Nelly and Nit

Nancy is a term of endearment much used by soccer fans as in 'Gerrof the pitch yer great fat nancy.'

Nelly is a substitute for Nancy.

Nit is a substitute for Nancy and Nelly.

Nets

Nets are what hang behind the goals to stop the crowd getting at the custodian. They have another function of stopping footballs, which nowadays is a secondary one. The sad fact is that modern soccer being what it is, the goalkeeper is more threatened from the rear than the front.

O is for . . .

Offside

Which is something your team never is.

Own Goal

Glancing through your Sunday newspaper at the triumphs and massacres of the previous day's matches you will see, listed beneath each published result, the names of the individual goal-scorers in the game, i.e.: Atkinson (1), Merryweather (1), Hoddinott o.g. And from this simple collection of names and numbers you may take it that Atkinson and Merryweather were the heroes of the game and that Hoddinott o.g. was a potential suicide. Hoddinott o.g. does not refer, as you might assume, to Hoddinott Old Grammarian, or even Oliver George Hoddinott. Hoddinott o.g. means Hoddinott own goal.

Hoddinott is one of those most unfortunate of men who has suffered the bleak misfortune of slotting the ball between his own posts. Hoddinott o.g. has scored a goal against his own side. In the sport of football with all its laughter and tears, fortune and sorrows, there is no crueller quirk that fate has to offer than to suffer the ignominy of the letters o.g. after one's name. Hoddinott o.g. is a man apart. Hoddinott o.g. is a social leper. Hoddinott o.g. is the one man in the world who *is* an island.

Hoddinott o.g. is usually a full-back. His fall from grace began with the best will in the world. Possibly, under pressure, he executed a perfectly correct and well-judged lob back, only to see it drift over his own goalkeeper's hands. Or perhaps he performed an elegant flying header in order to gain the respite of a justifiable corner-kick during a furious goal-mouth melee and then, in anguish, watched the ball flash between his own posts. Whatever his mistake, Hoddinott o.g. took no part in the comradely ribaldry of his team-mates after the match.

In the dressing-room and communal bath, when the final whistle had been blown, ten men laughed, joked, shared beakers of hot tea and pulled at the same cigarette. When the same ten men had bathed and changed and were drifting in twos and threes towards the players' bar, one man remained in the dressing-room, silent and still in the sweat of his football strip, only occasionally lifting his head from his hands to give it a mystified and unbelieving shake: Hoddinott o.g.

Own Goal means a lonely man.

P is for . . .

Paralytic

Paralytic is what players become after winning a cup final or being tackled by Norman Hunter.

Perks

See INDUCEMENT.

Public Address System

The Public Address System is the grand-sounding name for those half-dozen battered and crackling loudspeakers which are dotted around the ground. The Public Address System is put to many uses during the afternoon to enrich your pleasure and liven things up a bit when the game itself falls into its usual slough of boredom. To further increase your enjoyment, the loudspeakers are set at such intervals whereby the sound from one comes just one second later than the sound from the next, giving either an interesting and unusual echo effect or a totally indistinguishable jumble of noises.

The Public Address System breaks down frequently. (See TEAM)

On match days you will become aware of the Public Address System long before you arrive at the ground. Hours before kick-off time the loudspeakers blare out, over an approximate area of three square miles, a selection of tunes which the directors of the club, in their dotage, firmly believe to be the latest hits from the Top Ten – chart-stoppers such as Keep Right On To The End Of The Road,

Abide With Me, The Desert Song or, if you happen to be a Nottingham Forest Supporter – Robin Hood, Robin Hood, Marching Through The Glen.

Until a few seasons ago, the honour of making the announcements over the Public Address System was bestowed upon one of the directors of the club. The mantle of authority lay heavily upon his shoulders. He was invariably a middle-aged second-hand car dealer who spoke with a broad Midlands accent and delivered his pronouncements with the hushed authority and solemnity of a mortal man delegated to deliver the Sermon on the Mount. With a nervous tremor underlining the importance of his epoch-making announcements, he would come out with tit-bits such as: 'Will the owner of the blue mini, registration number KGB 463, please move it from the entrance to the main stand where it is blocking the access of the chairman's Bentley to the directors' car-park.' Or, 'If the hooligans at the Exley Road end persist in throwing pennies at the referee, the match will be abandoned.'

Over recent years, however, a less formal approach has crept into the handling of the P.A. System. The microphone these days is in the hands of the director's son, a toothy lad with a Georgie Best haircut who favours a more trendy approach and sees himself as a second Jimmy Savile. He adopts a hysterical tone of voice, gets far too close to the mike, and deafens his captive audience with his personal brand of Radio One-type script-writing:

'Wait for it, fans, it's the disc you've all been waiting for! And it's a personal request by our Maureen – yes! Miss Sludge United herself – the dee-lightful and dee-lectable Maureen Liversedge, popular Queen of the supporters' club, who I happen to know is in her usual position behind the goal!'

The delightful and delectable Maureen is a squat, spotty sixteen-year-old scrubber whose favourite position is flat on her back. She sports a scarf in the club colours embroidered with the christian names of all the first team, and spends her evenings behind the stand putting herself about with all the reserves.

The Public Address System is also used, after reserve games, to inform the handful of keen supporters who have attended how the first team have fared in their away fixture. If the reserves have gone down six–nil at home it serves as some small consolation to the disappointed stalwarts, gathered round the main speaker, when they hear that the first team had more success and were beaten by the narrower margin of five goals to nil.

Q is for . . .

Questionable Decision

A questionable decision is one awarded by a referee, against your team, inside your own penalty area.

For the sake of further enlightenment let us give an example. Supposing during a game your right full-back suffers a sudden attack of pins and needles in his leg. In order to alleviate the pain he sticks out his boot and waggles his foot. At the same time the silly billy-goat of an opposing centre-forward, not looking where he is going and concentrating only on the ball at his feet, trips over the outstretched boot, causing further hurt to your full-back. It will be generally agreed by your fellow-fans on the terraces that the muggins of a centre-forward has got his just deserts when he lands face-first in the mud. A good referee would have no hesitation in awarding a free-kick to your side for ungentlemanly conduct by the centre-forward. Quite right too. But a bad referee who has not kept up with the play might even be so foolish as to award a penalty against your team. This would be classified as a questionable decision and it will be obvious from the uproar of the crowd that the referee has boobed. After all, thirty-thousand level-headed spectators must know better than one referee!

There is no such thing as a questionable decision *against* the opposing team inside their own penalty area.

Quotes

Quotes are what sports reporters are supposed to get from football players. This exercise was once harshly summed up as being: 'People who can't write in pursuit of people who can't talk.' That is an unfair assessment of both journalists and soccer players but the fact remains that the majority of quotes from soccer players that appear in our national press appear to have been invented by the man who writes the jokes that go inside Christmas crackers. It is of course a difficult job getting quotes. Most sports editors demand that the players be interviewed after a game and it is easy to imagine the difficulties inherent in talking sense to someone who has just run his blood to water for ninety minutes, been abused by the crowd for his pains and moreover spotted his wife behind the goals with the milkman. In such circumstances even the gentlest enquiry as to his feelings and general well-being is likely to provoke a response which to say the least is unprintable. Which is why all players in that situation appear to give the same quote. It is not that they *do* say the same thing, it is simply that the experienced quote-hunter has the good sense to translate: 'Why don't you go and get —— you stupid —— ' as 'Well it was a hard game and the best team won.'

Until television came along it seemed likely that soccer players as represented in the press would go through life saying the same thing, but the camera in the dressing-room after the big game threatens to change all that. As yet the players and officials are guarded about television and only say the things that people expect them to say. But one day the breakthrough will come. One day a television reporter will approach a weary, defeated player as he trudges from the field and will ask him how he feels. And the player will tell him from the bottom of his heart and the tip of his tongue the real truth. It won't be a pretty sight, but it will be compulsory viewing.

R is for ...

Referee

If you look closely at the players as they come out of the tunnel and on to the pitch before the start of a game you will notice that amongst them are three men who, try as they may, cannot run quite as fast as the rest of the lads.

On closer inspection you will see that these three rather elderly gentlemen are wearing black rig-outs with dinky white celluloid collars and cuffs. Because of this strange clothing it is possible that you will mistake them for tea-shop waitresses, but a little reflection will confirm your suspicions that they are nothing of the kind (unless your team happens to be playing a friendly game against Lyons' Corner House).

These three gentlemen are the match officials, the referee and his two accomplice linesmen, specially selected and appointed by the Football Association to ensure that your lads stand the least possible chance of gaining a couple of points. There are thousands of appointed referees and linesmen up and down the country and, with growing conviction week by week, you will come to realise that each and every one of them has been recruited by the F.A. primarily because he bears a personal grudge against your side.

Match days apart, many referees are quite sane and responsible citizens, quite a number of them hold down respectable jobs – but not one of them is willing to declare in public his biased interest in the game. Only on Saturday afternoons and at evening floodlit matches do these men reveal themselves in their true colours and announce to the spectators what a rotten, ignorant pig-headed lot they really are. In order that you should not recognise them during their non-refereeing hours, all referees adopt a simple disguise tactic during the match: they take off their glasses.

'PUT YOUR GLASSES ON REF!' is a cry which you will hear again and again during the course of a single season. Whenever this heart-rending appeal deafens your ear on the terraces you will know that yet another referee has had his disguise penetrated by one of his workmates or neighbours.

Every schoolboy in the land can reel off the five necessary articles which the referee is called upon to carry out onto the field with him, as listed in the football code. Few schoolboys are aware of the real use to which the referee puts these articles:

1. THE MATCH-BALL. Before the game a referee is offered the choice of several footballs. He will always select the one which is over-pumped and consequently will not bounce true. Your own side, proficient footballers that you know them to be, will find the badly bouncing ball to their disadvantage. On the other hand, the opposing team are always such a rotten lot of clumsy donkeys that it would not make one jot of difference to them if the referee was to run out on the pitch with a cabbage under his arm.

2. A PENNY. Supposedly for the purpose of ensuring a fair start to the game when tossed up by the two opposing captains to give the choice of ends or kick-off. After you have been to three or four games however, you will quickly realise that your captain never wins the toss and hardly any thought at all will provide the reason – the coin the referee produces is a double-headed one. The opposing captain always gets his shout in first in order to take advantage of this sneaky ruse; your own team leader, honest and sporting chap that he is, will not stoop to such underhanded deceits.

3 and 4. A NOTEBOOK AND PENCIL. Two articles that the referee carries in his pocket in order to jot down the name of any player in your team who accidentally jostles or gives a friendly nudge to one of his opponents, your player's name

then being forwarded to the F.A. for disciplinary action. Once your player has had his name taken, for absolutely no reason, he will be unnerved for the remainder of the game. Again, should one of your players make the ultimate mistake of touching an opponent, with no more than his little finger, inside your own penalty area, the offended cry-baby will at once leap four feet into the air, fall down flat on his face and lie there pretending dead for as long a period as suits his purpose. On such occasions the referee spurns the use of his notebook and pencil and points dramatically to that instrument of goalkeepers' torture known as the penalty spot. On the other hand, if any number of the opposing team ferociously attack one of your players with head and boot and fist inside *their* penalty area, the referee will flail his arms in the air ineffectually, thus signalling that he has noticed the incident but, as the opposing centre-half is his brother-in-law, he does not propose to take any action.

5. A STOP-WATCH. Which should be used, in theory, to time the ninety allotted minutes of play, but which, in fact, is a mechanical device issued to referees so that they can add precious minutes to a match, particularly when your team is struggling to hold down a one-nil lead after ninety minutes spent ankle-deep in mud away from home.

Apart from the official items listed the referee, and both the linesmen, carry on to the field with them their deep enmity against your club and a bitter hatred in their hearts for each and every member of your playing staff.

S is for . . .

Seltick

See SASSENACH MIS-SPELLING.

Sex

Which doesn't mix with Soccer. (See COLD SHOWER)

Striker

A striker is simply the modern term for what used to be known as a centre-forward. His job is to put the ball in the net using his head, feet and any other part of the anatomy apart from his hands which are only used when the referee isn't looking. Because they score goals and because goals are the currency of soccer, strikers are transferred for vast amounts of money, and the best strikers are simply priceless. There is the story told of one manager who rang another to see if he could buy a great goalscorer. He said: 'I'll pay you £250,000 for him.' To which the other manager replied: 'That sounds O.K. Which particular game did you want him to play in?' To do the job properly, strikers must be tall and blessed with a formidable technique. In addition to having strapping thighs and bulging biceps they also need something not normally taken into account when assessing an athlete's equipment, namely a forehead so constructed that it can withstand a lifetime's contact with a football. It is often said of a person that he has muscles in his head. Directed at the normal person this would be a highly derogatory remark deserving of a knuckle sandwich. Used in relation to a striker it is a huge compliment. The ideal

forehead for a striker was invented by Baron Frankenstein for his famous monster. Had the Baron been alive today he could have made a fortune producing strikers for football clubs. (Just one more sad case of misguided genius.)

Because he spends much of his working life sticking his head in front of fast-moving footballs the striker is unlikely to be included in any list of well-known intellectuals. The fact is of course that any intelligent and sensitive person would never become a striker in the first place. Any cool appraisal of the hazards of the job would place it somewhere on a level with lion taming and only just below diving over Niagara Falls in a barrel of concrete.

What the striker lacks in intelligence he more than compensates for in raw courage. He spends all his working life in that murderous patch of green called the penalty area which is something like working in a snake pit. He is guarded by defenders whose ruthless dedication to the job of preventing goals being scored only just stops short of murder. The next time you see a striker rise out of the penalty area and glide a football off his forehead into the corner of the net do not marvel how it was done, but marvel that it was done at all. It is likely that before he leapt for the ball the striker had been punched in the kidneys, kicked on the ankles, kneed in the back and rabbit-punched below the left ear. Moreover as he jumped for the ball he was more than likely leaving earth with two thirteen stone athletes hanging on to his shirt tails. Every working day of their lives strikers are supposed to suffer this kind of undignified treatment and score goals of precision and grace. That they often achieve it under these handicaps is a classic example of great art under severe duress.

From all that has gone before it will be realised that strikers are born and not made and that there aren't many of them around. Fathers should inspect their sons at an early age for the physical characteristics that can be turned into gold. If the baby has a forehead like Ludwig Von Beethoven and legs like Rudolph Nureyev he should contact his local football manager immediately. Strikers might be made in heaven but they are treasured most here on earth.

Strip

Should it ever fall to your good fortune to actually hold a conversation with a real footballer, in person, he might make passing reference to his strip. You must not assume from this that he is talking about his young lady who works in Soho and takes off her clothes eight or nine times a day for a crust of bread – if a footballer refers to his strip he is talking about the clothes he wears to play football in.

When a player arrives at the ground before a game he first inspects the pitch and then decides which boots (long studs, short studs or moulded rubber soles), will best suit the playing conditions. He then repairs to the dressing-room where his shirt, shorts and stockings have been laid out for him, freshly laundered, on his very own peg. It is then that the pre-match ritual begins. And if it is your belief that before a footballer appears in front of his admiring fans it is, for him, a simple matter of donning boots and clean linen, then you have still got an awful lot to learn about football.

If you could see your hero before the game, primping and preening himself in the dressing-room, you might easily imagine that you had entered the changing quarters of the England Ladies Hockey team; for the unguents and toiletries that a player daubs on his body before a game are to be seen to be believed. Did you know, for example, that before your virile champion trots out on to the pitch he has vaselined his eyebrows, oiled his body, embrocated his legs and greased his stockinged feet?

'Hold hard!' you exclaim. 'Why, in God's good name, has he *greased* his stockinged feet?' Well may you ask. Although, in the player's favour, it should be pointed out that he has not applied the grease to the pair of stockings next to his skin.

'Halt! Enough!' You cry for a second time. 'Are you suggesting that the player wears *more* than one pair of stockings?' Indeed he does, because his boots are too big. And if you are wondering why the half-dozen millionaires who call themselves your board of directors don't buy the players boots which fit them, it is because the players actually prefer to play in boots that are too big. It gives them the opportunity to wear two pairs of stockings.

Footballers, generally speaking, are a funny lot of chaps.

Suicidal Tendencies

Suicidal tendencies are common to every football fan who has seen his team relegated and every forward who ever missed an open goal.

Sunday Football

Sunday footballers comprise that innumerable army of lads sufficiently enthusiastic and mad-headed enough to turn out in hurricane or snowstorm every Sunday morning or on any evening in the week when they are lucky enough to arrange (a), a fixture and (b), a ground luxuriating in the glory of either a workable floodlight system or a close proximity to a motorway lighting complex.

Closely aligned in spirit to the Sunday footballer is a small and select band of Italian waiters who are readily available for week-day afternoon fixtures outside of restaurant opening hours, but they are hard put to find any sort of opposition and are usually to be found moodily kicking balls about by themselves in parks and open public spaces.

The true Sunday footballer will turn out on any ground no matter what the conditions: from a pitch the size of a miniature tennis court to a ploughed field with an incline approximating to an Alpine ski-slope. The Sunday footballer is a gregarious creature with a natural herd instinct. If you stand at any bus-stop in the United Kingdom at ten o'clock on a Sunday morning, a pair of football boots under your arm, it's an odds on certainty that within ten minutes you will have been joined by a full team of similar hopefuls, plus a substitute and a trainer in a bowler hat who will have a dozen helpful suggestions as to where a game may be had.

The prime difference between the Sunday footballer and his Saturday counterpart, skills apart, is one of age. The average pro player's career span is between the ages of eighteen and thirty-five – the Sunday footballer begins playing serious competitive football at the age of six, and if not dissuaded by his nearest and dearest is quite capable of continuing in the game until arthritis and/or rheumatism forbids him the ability to bend down and lace up his boots.

A league football club has its own supporters' club and extensive ground facilities. The Sunday football team has a couple of shivering fiancees and one disillusioned wife with a washing machine and a clothes-line long enough to take eleven football shirts. Whereas the pro club has changing rooms and modern baths, the Sunday lads share the back seat of a Mini Minor for a dressing-room and have grudging access to the gents lav at the local boozer.

But Sunday football has one great advantage over the pro game for the spectator enthusiast: while the supporter of a First Division team will often stand on a wind-swept terrace for ninety minutes and then trudge home after a goal-less draw, the follower of a Sunday side rarely leaves a match without seeing his team win or lose by the narrow margin of the odd thirteen goals.

For the spectator interested in pursuing the possibilities of Sunday football, it should also be pointed out that the chances of attaining promotion to the list of club officials are much more open than for the average Saturday supporter. A football fan who follows a pro side often devotes a life-time of service to his club giving fervent support from behind the goal without ever once being invited to become a director, assume the managerial chair for a season, or even be invited into the board-room at half-time for a cup of tea and a ginger biscuit. The football enthusiast who gives himself to the Sunday game is almost certain to be invited to take on the post of president of the club if he so much as watches a whole game from start to finish. Should he accept the burden of office he will immediately enjoy all the perks which go with the position: first name familiarities with all the players, the opportunity of carrying the magic sponge or the touch-judge's flag, and the chance to invest in the ten bob whip in the boozer after the final whistle.

For the football fan who seeks the ultimate in recognition from his pursuance of the delights of Sunday soccer, both from his club and in the columns of the local press, it is recommended that he position himself outside his nearest league club on a Saturday afternoon during a home game. When the ball is miskicked out of the ground he must snatch it up and hare for home. His local sports reporter, also a Sunday football fanatic, will duly record in his weekly piece on the amateur soccer scene:

> 'THE MATCH-BALL FOR SUNDAY'S GAME, WORSLEY AND BICKERSTHORPE CASUALS VERSUS GRIMLEY KNITTING MACHINES F.C., WAS KINDLY DONATED BY MR REGINALD HAVERTHWAITE, A PROMINENT LOCAL SPORTSMAN.'

Superstition

Footballers, to a man, are as superstitious as a wagon-load of Cornish Pixies. They believe in their lucky pitches, their lucky Saturdays, their lucky charms and their lucky referees.

A player will wear the same pair of boots, season after season until they fall apart on the field, because he believes them to possess some sort of mystical power. The same player will spend half an hour in the dressing-room before the game lacing the same pair of boots in an intricate network of crossings and uncrossings, knowing it to be lucky. Another player will give his team-mates a pre-match acrobatic display in an attempt to put on his jock-strap over his head, firmly believing that unless he succeeds the game is as good as lost. Some players believe it is lucky for them to put their shirts on before their shorts, others believe the opposite.

There are players who believe that their individual luck will hold if they can be last man out onto the pitch – the story is told of two such players, in a Sunday League match, who found themselves on the same side and spent the first half of the game glaring at each other across the dressing-room while the rest of their team played forty-five minutes with nine men.

It has yet to be proved that any of these fads, foibles and fancies are of the slightest use. A player can turn out on his lucky day, playing on his lucky pitch, wearing his lucky boots and his lucky talisman, under the supervision of his lucky referee – and trudge off the field after the match having been on the receiving end of a seven-nil thrashing. He will accept the defeat philosophically and explain it away by saying that seven is his unlucky number.

Players are nothing if not loyal to their superstitions.

T is for . . .

Team

The team, the actual playing side, the eleven good lads and true upon whom all your hopes and dreams are founded when the kick-off whistle blows, is selected by the manager on the evening preceding the match day. These are the chaps (plus substitute), whose duty it is to uphold the honour of the club, secure two valuable points, clog the opposition into the ground, and confirm your own pride and belief in them in the nearest saloon bar after the game.

It is the manager's task to sift and select from among his playing staff the cream of the footballing potential. The final decision and the resultant victory or failure rests solely on your manager's shoulders – bear with him. When he chooses his players he will take into account match-fitness, playing skill, balance in the side and individual confidence – although if a manager is running a Sunday football team, a player may well be selected simply because he owns (or is in a position to beg, borrow or steal), a pair of football boots.

The eleven selected players together make up a heterogeneous collection of strikers, forwards, midfield players, defenders and one goalkeeper who will be instantly recognisable from the rest by his gloves, cap, different coloured jersey and butter-fingers.

With the exception of the goalkeeper, the lads are individually distinguishable by the numbers which they carry either on the back of their jerseys or, continental style, on the front of their shorts. The latter system being much favoured by clogging defenders and other hard-men who use it to advantage to hide their identity from the referee by the simple process of wearing their shirts outside their shorts and pulling them well down over the numbers, thus negating the original reason for wearing numbers anyway.

Once the teams have trotted out on to the pitch for their pre-match kick-about, a glance at your programme will immediately establish that the names listed therein bear little or no resemblance to the individuals who are out on the ground. Don't be surprised. Last minute programme alterations are an integral part of the sport of football and are normally employed by managers to provide lively debatable material for the fans on the terraces. Take advantage of this opportunity and engage the man standing next to you in conversation. 'Why the effin' 'ell is that great donkey playing at centre-half?' is a promising opening gambit for earnest argument, probably drawing forth the reply, 'Who the effin' 'ell do you think should play at centre-half?' And immediately you are off on a sound footing for a keen and intelligent discussion.

Having discovered from your programme that the eleven chaps who have gone out to do battle in your name are total strangers to you, keep your eyes skinned for an aged, bald-headed chap in wellington boots who will hare round the pitch, shortly before the kick-off, holding aloft a blackboard chalked with hieroglyphics.

The appearance of this ancient may be taken as a sign that the Public Address System has broken down. (See PUBLIC ADDRESS SYSTEM)

The chalk-marks on the greybeard's blackboard, which you will not be able to decipher, are very important. They quite probably relate to the last-minute team changes. If you are sufficiently fortunate to be standing next to a fellow supporter who possesses 40/40 eyesight and a degree in the Ancient Egyptian language, beg from him a literal translation. Your educated companion will give you a breakdown of numbers which may, or on the other hand may not, bear some relation to the identity of the players and the numbers on their shirts or shorts. This could be quite complicated.

If the number is 12 or below, you can safely assume that it has something to do with the playing side. If the number is in the region of 13 to 30,000 you may assume that it refers to a lucky programme number or a Penny On The Ball ticket. Check your personal belongings. If the number on the blackboard coincides with the number stamped on your programme, take it to the club secretary's office. You will be presented with the unique opportunity of obtaining two free tickets to the next home game – your team may go down by thirteen goals to nil, but it will not cost you a penny to watch the game. Similarly, should the number on the blackboard coincide with one on the cloakroom ticket which was foisted on you at the turnstile for no apparent reason, present that ticket at the secretary's office and it will be your good fortune to take home to your wife a soaking, mud-spattered, spherical piece of plastic coated leather. Woman that she is, she will not appreciate it. She would have preferred flowers or a box of chocolates. In any case, either of the above contingencies is extremely unlikely but they have served their purpose and passed the time prior to the actual game.

Let us now assume that the referee has supervised the toss-up, the opposing captains have shaken hands, with each other and with the referee, the players take up their positions for the start of the match.

As your lads range themselves across their half of the pitch, before the referee blows his whistle to commence play, you will be able to assess, from the positions they have taken up, the formation in which your team has elected to play: four–three–three, four–two–four, two–three–five or, in the event of a difficult away fixture, nine full-backs and an optimistic goal-poacher. Whichever of these systems has been chosen, you may be sure that the decision to play it has not been taken lightly. Your manager has spent most of the week studying and calculating the methods of the opposition; assessing his own players' capabilities and deploying them to their best advantage.

He has been wasting his time.

Once the referee blows up for the game to start, twenty robust lads will scurry about the pitch for ninety full minutes willy-nilly like a herd of agile sheep, while the two goal-keepers hurl obscenities at their own team-mates from their stationary view-point between the posts. This is what you have paid good money to see. If you take your eyes from this shambles for a moment and glance down at the trainer's bench you will see that your team manager is sitting with his head in his hands. He may even be crying. He feels exactly the same as you. It is possible that, at that moment, you may feel sympathy and compassion for him. Think twice, at least he is getting paid to be there.

Television Commentator

A television commentator is someone who describes an incident you have just seen for yourself. The difference between what he saw and what you saw is that he gets the names wrong. Many people lust after the television commentator's job and everyone thinks he can do the job better, which is why television commentators are shy, withdrawn men who live in the country behind high walls and don't have their number in the local telephone directory.

Next to referees, television commentators are the favourite objects of the fans' abuse. If they make a single mistake in a commentary lasting ninety minutes they are labelled as cretins by the armchair critics. If they hazard an interpretation of a team's tactics they are called an ignorant fool by a million embryo Alf Ramseys, each of whom believes that he knows more about football than any man living. If the commentator lets the game speak for itself and only uses his voice sparingly, he is accused of shirking his duty, if on the other hand he describes every move, interprets every incident he automatically becomes a loud-mouthed twit. Like referees, television commentators are born losers, they just cannot win. Again like referees, theirs is the classic instance of power without respect.

Tickets

Tickets are issued for big games like Cup Finals to enable people who are not interested in football to get the best seats.

Tight-Marking

A tight-marking player is one whose prime skill is that of being able to crack the shins of the opposing forwards without getting his name taken by the referee.

Time-Wasting

Time-wasting is a disgraceful and unsportsmanlike practice whereby a team, leading in a match by the odd goal or struggling to hold down a draw during the last vital minutes of a hard away fixture, employ various devious means to squander vital seconds of play, such as by booting the ball over the popular stand or by standing with a foot on the ball by the opposition's corner flag.

The phrase time-wasting has only crept into the game over the last few seasons before which it was commonly known as wasting time, which doesn't sound half so bad and consequently nobody bothered about it very much.

Toe-End

Toe-End is what players used to give the ball in the days when boots had toe-ends. Today footballers wear slippers on their feet and the language of soccer has lost a gem.

Toilet Facilities

There is a lack of toilet facilities at football grounds. Most soccer clubs work on the principle that one hole in the ground is sufficient for sixty thousand people. One day they will be proved wrong in the most disastrous way imaginable and no one who has queued from half-time to the final whistle to answer the call of nature will shed a tear.

The reason why toilets on special soccer trains are attacked by fans is that they have never seen one before.

Touts

Touts are people who are pleased when tickets are issued for big games. They all have little black contact books full of names of people who wouldn't be seen dead behind the goals at Highbury but who would pay thirty quid to see the Queen at Wembley.

Training

Training is how the players pass their time learning skills and raising themselves to the peak of fitness for five mornings of every week at all professional football clubs. Semi-professional footballers have other employments during the day and their training is confined to evenings, twice a week. Training is where Sunday footballers tell their wives and girl-friends they are going when, in fact, they are meeting their mates in the boozer or taking dodgy birds to the cinema.

Professional footballers train very hard. From Monday to Friday they run, skip, jump, lift heavy weights and do all manner of exercises from half-past nine in the morning until it is time to break for lunch. It is because they train so hard during the week that they always seem so tired every Saturday afternoon.

...OVER TRAINED....

Professional footballers also attend tactical sessions which are held to iron out the mistakes they were guilty of during the previous Saturday's match. The club's manager and the team coach sit down with the eager lads and talk through the errors and faults that were committed, discuss the reasons and decide how the mistakes can be put to rights in future games. In order that the players may better understand, the mistakes are demonstrated on a magnetic board, painted to represent a football pitch, with the aid of little plastic men. Afterwards, when the players have seen and understood the error of their ways, they go out and practise the corrected moves themselves on the pitch. These moves are gone over again and again and again, until manager, coach and each individual player is satisfied and sure that that particular mistake will not be made again. The following Saturday the players trot out on the pitch and do the selfsame thoughtless daft stupid trick. This is why you will often see a manager sitting on the trainer's bench with his head in his hands.

Professional footballers do not train in the afternoons because many of them are very rich and have outside business interests, such as owning restaurants or boutiques or laying linoleum. The players who are not so rich spend most of their afternoons in betting shops.

Trendy

Certain teams become trendy at some point in their history. Fulham used to be trendy but that ended when they went into the Third Division. Spurs were trendy when they had a great team but nowadays are out of fashion. The trendiest club at present is Chelsea which is not bad consolation for a team which used to be a music-hall joke.

To be trendy, a club must attract to its games a lot of showbiz people who wear spectacular clothes and talk nonsense about soccer in very loud voices. As these people always follow success and live in the Kings Road it will be deduced that quite naturally the trendy teams will always be found in London, preferably south of the river. There is no danger of Rotherham United ever becoming trendy.

U is for . . .

Ungentlemanly Conduct and Unseemly Behaviour

Ungentlemanly conduct encompasses a curious collection of misdemeanours which no male person of good breeding would ever dream of committing. Crimes such as petulantly booting the ball off the pitch, leaving the pitch without the referee's permission, hiding the ball up the back of one's jumper and looking innocently around while the referee is waiting to get on with the game, all these come under the heading of UNGENTLEMANLY CONDUCT. While, surprisingly, crimes such as calling the referee names or spitting at a linesman are not considered ungentlemanly and are punishable under separate headings. (See VIOLENCE OF THE TONGUE)

UNSEEMLY BEHAVIOUR is to the fans what UNGENTLEMANLY CONDUCT is to the players. UNSEEMLY BEHAVIOUR is the bad manners of the terraces. The curious thing about UNSEEMLY BEHAVIOUR is that no official code appears to have been laid down and it is interesting to note the infringements that you, as a fan, *can* get away with in these days of strict police control.

You CAN get away with throwing lavatory paper at the opposition's goal-mouth (in the entire history of football nobody has ever been imprisoned for this offence), provided it cannot be proved that you stole the toilet roll from the Board of Directors' lavatory.

You CAN get away with attending any league ground in the country in steel-capped, hob-nailed bother-boots, always provided that you are willing to leave them in the safe keeping of the gentleman at the turnstile until after the game. From the middle of November until the end of March it is advisable to take a pair of carpet slippers in your raincoat pocket.

You CANNOT get away with entering any ground with a cudgel, blunt instrument or walking-stick, even though in the latter case you may be affecting a heavy limp and claim to be suffering the after-effects of a skiing holiday in Kitzbuhl (although with an excuse as good as that you could get into the ground in an invalid carriage or wheel-chair and watch the game in comfort from the touch-lines).

You CANNOT get away with invading the pitch at any league game, although a certain laxity is allowed at cup-ties when you will be escorted from the field of play by a friendly policeman but allowed to remain on the terraces until the final whistle. In the case of a Cup Final the decision as to whether or not you are turfed from the ground seems to rest with the individual constable, although it's well worth taking a chance as you are likely to be immortalised before the entire nation on Colour T.V. If it happens to be a dull, plodding goal-less Cup Final your antics may even be repeated in slow-motion on the instant replay cameras.

You CANNOT get away with taking an empty bottle, concealed about your person, into any ground in the country, but in the case of a bottle still containing liquid refreshment opinion would seem to be divided – for example, no man in kilt and tam-o-shanter has ever been denied access to an International fixture on the grounds that he was carrying a bottle of Scotch in his sporran.

You CANNOT get away with anything when it comes to insulting a police-horse. The British are very hot about this kind of thing.

All in all you will find that the unwritten rules vary up and down the country but, for your own peace of mind, it would be wise if you were to memorise the above do's and don'ts. UNSEEMLY BEHAVIOUR is punishable at all levels, ranging from a light fine to long imprisonment or, worst of all, being banned from your local ground and therefore committed to a lifetime of Saturday afternoons spent watching Cyclo-Cross, Gymnastics and All-In-Wrestling on television. Although, in the latter case, there is some slight consolation

in that you do get to see the football results as they come over the teleprinter. This means that you can be down in the boozer celebrating your eight score-draws while the rest of the lads are still in the crush at the ground, struggling to get out of the main gates.

V is for . . .

Victory

V is for Victory, or the sweet smell of success which will give your champions another two valuable points in the urgent fight for promotion or the bitter struggle against relegation. V is for Victory, which could ensure that your favourites will live to play again in the next round of the knock-out competition which leads, ultimately, to that which all men dream about, the Holy Grail – otherwise known as the F.A. Cup.

There are two kinds of victories – those that are achieved on your own ground and those that are won on an away midden. Of the two, the second is by far the sweeter, and also far more dangerous where your own personal well-being is concerned. Should it be your good fortune to be present on an alien ground on a day when your heroes bring off an away win you will be well advised to act modestly – at least until you get to the nearest railway station. As you leave the ground, tuck your rosette in an inside pocket and stuff your rattle inside your raincoat, walk casually though purposefully as if you were strolling around the familiar back-streets of your own town. If, by chance, you are accosted by one of the home supporters attempt to copy his accent and share his disappointment.

Do not, under any circumstances, make sport of his team's lack of success. Be a sportsman. 'Hard luck, mate! You deserved at least a point!' These simple words, coupled with a friendly wave of the hand, will go a long way towards getting you home with most of your teeth intact.

On the other hand, should you win at home, you are fully entitled to enjoy your victory to the final ounce and give vent to your true feelings. 'What a load of old scrubbers!' or 'Go

"...GETTING HOME WITH MOST OF YOUR TEETH INTACT"

home, you twots, go home!' sung jeeringly at an opposing supporter trudging his way from the ground will give you immense satisfaction when mob-handed.

In the event of an away win you may find yourself drawn to join the band of fellow supporters, on average twelve-year-olds, which gathers outside the players' entrance, waiting to cheer the team as it boards the coach. In which case you will be rewarded by actually being allowed to touch your personal hero, congratulating him with a gentle slap on the back or an assuring squeeze of his upper arm, while murmuring the words, 'Bloody well done, lad!' or 'They were never in the game!' And almost certainly you will receive in return from your champion a smile, a nod, or even a wink. This touching little exchange may result in your missing the last train home and spending the night on a bleak and unfriendly railway station – but it will be infinitely worth your while.

In the event of a home win it is more than likely that you will be borne off, by the supporters around you, to a celebration in the nearest boozer. You must take it for granted that you will be expected to remain there until closing time and, if the landlord of the hostelry is also a fan of your team, well into the early hours of the morning, locked in the bar parlour singing I'm Forever Blowing Bubbles or, We Are The Champions! Take heart. Sing up! Enter into the pervading spirit of camaraderie. And whatever else you may do, for goodness sake don't keep glancing at your watch, shuffling your feet and muttering under your breath about previous dinner dates or half-made promises to take your wife to the pictures.

Today is *your* day. Enjoy it to the full. Remember that next week, by the law of averages, it is quite within the bounds of possibility that your team might *lose*.

Surely that good and gentle little woman who took you for better or worse is not entirely without understanding? Don't underestimate the girl's feelings. And if (and occasionally it has been *known* to happen), the lady that you love more than anything in the world except football, does not fully comprehend your passion for the game, don't despair. All is not yet lost.

When you do finally stagger home at two or three in the morning, carry with you a copy of your local evening classified newspaper headlining your team's success. Then, as you trip over the landing carpet and fall into the bedroom, where your wife will be laying in wait to greet you, wave your newspaper above your head and bellow, *a la* Bobby Charlton, 'How about *that* then!' And your good lady, sensing the scent of victory in your demeanour, will immediately assume a prone position and pretend to be fast asleep. It is possible that recriminations will follow at breakfast but who are you to worry about that?

When the chips are down, Victory is what the game is all about.

And, if you are one of those unfortunates whose team happens to be playing so badly at the moment that you can't remember what Victory feels like, cheer up. It'll come. Your lads may be propping up the Fourth Division. Perhaps you went down ten–nil last week at home.

Change is just round the corner. When next Saturday comes

and the front door slams behind you, wear your favour bravely, stride down the street with your head held high. Walk on, walk on with hope in your heart and, as the Liverpool fans at Anfield Road will tell you – You'll Never Walk Alone.

Violence of the Tongue

VIOLENCE OF THE TONGUE is not, as it might sound, a fifteenth century form of punishment for witchcraft or a Chinese method of torture. VIOLENCE OF THE TONGUE is an offence against the football code committed by players on the field of play. VIOLENCE OF THE TONGUE usually means that a footballer has muttered to the referee's face the four letter word that thirty-odd thousand fans have been yelling at him all afternoon. Referees are inclined to frown upon VIOLENCE OF THE TONGUE and usually invite the offending player to leave the pitch and wash out his mouth with soap and water – thus originating the phrase 'going off for an early shower'.

GOING OFF FOR AN EARLY SHOWER...

W is for . . .

War

See WORLD CUP.

Wembley Stadium

To the vast following of the biggest spectator sport in the country, Wembley Stadium is the Mecca of football, the scene for the confrontation of the giants in the League Cup, the glorious battlefield where the England team take on their continental challengers, the Rome to which all roads lead in the F.A. Cup.

To the vast following of the second biggest spectator sport in the country, Wembley Stadium is a dog-track. It depends which way you look at things.

Wife Beating

Wife Beating is one way of getting it out of your system when the lads lose. According to social anthropologists, the custom is more prevalent in the industrial north than in the home counties. Often the wife is beaten only after the cat has been kicked and the tea thrown in the fireback. Allied to cat kicking and tea chucking, wife beating is nothing more than a quaint ritual signifying one man's passion for the game. Practised as a solo sport, which is to say that the wife gets beaten but the cat is unhurt and the tea gets eaten, it becomes something else and constitutes reasonable grounds for divorce. In the genuine soccer fan, substitutes for wife beating, cat kicking, etc., are difficult to suggest. Some men have tried drink, others have gone on drugs. Both create more problems than they warrant. We suggest you try the chapter heading in this book marked *S* for SUICIDE TENDENCIES and *C* for CRICKET.

Wogs

Wogs are chaps who play football but don't speak English. Wogs used to be people who didn't play soccer as well as the English but a few years ago some Hungarian wogs came to Wembley and thrashed the English and since that time quite a few wogs have shown themselves to be as good, if not better, than we are. Nowadays we play a lot of soccer against the wogs, but it would be wrong to interpret this as a laudatory example of sport building bridges between nations.

The fact is that we play wogs because there is money in it. The discovery that roubles, drachma, marks, lire and francs can be exchanged for real money at the Bank of England caused us to revise our thinking about playing wogs. But even though we take their money we still think they are inferior. What is very curious is that although the British generally, and British sportsmen in particular deride the wogs and wouldn't let their daughters marry one, they have in fact adopted a lot of wog fashions in both dress and behaviour. Take the question of soccer strip for example. It was British soccer that gave the world floppy shirts, baggy pants, shin pads like fire-guards and cast iron boots with bulbous toes. Yet nowadays every British team has rejected this uniform in favour of the indecently streamlined apparel invented by the wogs. Similarly it used to be that British soccer players would never dream of kissing one another in front of sixty thousand people. That was something we left to the wogs. Nowadays the scene on any British football ground at three o'clock on a Saturday afternoon when someone has scored resembles a love-in and is enough to make real men weep. Furthermore the British soccer supporter has picked up the nastier habits of his continental cousins. It is sad to see people who gave the world the boo whistling their contempt as they do in France or Italy or other unspeakable countries like those.

However there are, thank God, some differences remaining. You can still tell the difference between an English soccer player and a wog by the manner in which he commits a foul. The wogs specialise in sneaky fouling like body-checking, shirt tugging and ankle tapping. The British player still sticks to those honest fouls we gave the world like going in over the top, tackling from behind and the good old kick on the kneecap. Moreover the wogs specialise in this dirty habit of spitting at opponents while the British remain true to a right cross to the chin end.

Those suckers who preach international brotherhood and extol the virtues of Britain joining the Common Market should know that whatever happens the soccer players will remain true to their birthright and treat the foreign foe as bloody wogs.

World Cup

The World Cup is a four-yearly orgy when the nations of the world meet to kick lumps off one another. The winners of the World Cup can call themselves world champions but in truth they are nothing of the sort. The fact of the matter is that the World Cup is more often decided not by a player's skill but by his adaptability to physical conditions. Thus when England won the World Cup in 1966 it was not because they were the best team in the competition but possibly because they were used to playing in British weather. Altitude problems at this year's World Cup in Mexico meant that the favourites were the teams whose players had three lungs apiece. Similarly, when in some future time the World Cup is played at Rekjavik, who dare say that Iceland will not be firm favourites?. And it would be a very misguided soul who didn't put his money on the Ghurkas when the event takes place in the foothills of the Himalayas.

All else apart World Cups bring out the worst in people of all races and creeds. Chauvinism runs riot. During the course of the competition the world stands in peril as nations aggravate their political differences on the greensward. The only consolation is that the Yanks don't play soccer. If they did there is little doubt that World War Three would have already happened and been caused by an offside decision.

X is for . . .

Xenophobia

See WOGS.

Y is for . . .

Young Footballers

A young footballer comes into his own on the day when his eager father arrives on the doorstep of the maternity hospital with a spanking new football underneath his arm. A young footballer is a bouncing boy who has reached an age when he has left the womb, but has not as yet arrived at that stage of maturity when he can grip a pen and write his name legibly on any amateur or professional forms which may be thrust in front of him.

Whereas an old footballer is one who, because of his declining years and fumbling arthritic fingers, can no longer cope with the intricacies of doing up his boots; a young footballer is a toddler who may possess many of the footballing skills (tackling, heading, dribbling, speed and agility), but who has not yet arrived at that age of consent when he is allowed to fasten his own boot-laces.

Young footballers are inclined to adopt the titles of their particular favourites as their own, and any male parent who is advised by his six-year-old son that he had been selected to represent Leeds United in a match against Real Madrid on the following Saturday morning must not leap to the assumption that his offspring's talents have at last been recognised by Don Revie. He may however take pride in the fact that his lad has had greatness thrust upon him and has been chosen to play in a Saturday morning juvenile kick-about in which he will be defending the honour of his nursery school playmates, his street, or his Bible-thumping Methodist Sunday School-fellows.

Young footballers are to be observed in all parks and on all open spaces on any Saturday morning, fifty-two weeks of the year. (Because of their unflagging enthusiasm, young footballers are not required by the Football Association to observe the Close Season.)

If selected to turn out in a Saturday morning kick-about, a young footballer is obliged to bring with him not only his boots and his father, but also his own shirt, stockings and shorts and also a jacket or anorak for use as a goal-post.

Young footballers progress from parks football, through junior, schools and youth teams, to an age and ability when they may be taken on as apprentices at professional football clubs. This is the goal of every proud father whose heart is in football. Given several years of football schooling, an apprentice becomes adept in the arts of cleaning first team players' boots, scrubbing out the baths and showers, and running down to the betting shop with the club manager's cross-doubles.

A word of warning to ambitious fathers. It must be accepted, from birth, that all children are not born players. For example, a promising young footballer will never make the grade for England selection if it is unfortunate enough to have been born a girl. Similarly, any robust lad of eleven or twelve who spurns his birthday football and turns for plaything to his dollies' house or Knitting Jenny is not to be considered as likely football material. A wise father will recognise the danger signs and put such a lad's name down for ballet school or art classes.

Z is for . . .

Zigger-Zagger

ZIGGER-ZAGGER is a chant, a chant is a hymn, a hymn is a song of praise. What better then, than to go out next Saturday afternoon and lift up your voice in praise of your own team? The tune is unimportant, the words are easy enough to learn:

Zigger-zagger, zigger-zagger, zigger-zagger,
Zigger-zagger, zigger-zagger, zigger-zagger,
Zigger-zagger, zigger-zagger, zigger-zagger,
Zigger-zagger, zigger-zagger, zigger-zagger.
(Repeat)

Congratulations, you have learnt your first football song. There are, of course, many others: GOD SAVE OUR GRACIOUS TEAM, and WE ARE THE CHAMPIONS, and WE SHALL NOT BE MOVED, and OUR SIDE ONE YOUR SIDE NIL HALLELUJAH, and WE'LL SUPPORT YOU EVERMORE, and GO HOME YOU TWOTS GO HOME. All these and lots more have now fallen into public domain. But it is not intended, in this book, to copy out a list of choruses. After all, this is not a volume of bawdy rugger songs. Soccer is not bawdy. Soccer is not uncouth. It is true that many football chants contain four letter words but, unlike the sniggering verses of the rugby oafs, they are never used with any sexual connotation. In Association football, the true intent of foul language is that of honest insult and pure abuse. They may be words that, previously, have not come easy to your lips. Take heart, they are the words of Chaucer and of Shakespeare. Common, simple words. Words of the English language. *Your* language. The language of the country that, way back in nineteen-sixty-six, took on the rest of the football world and emerged triumphant with the Jules Rimet Cup. Be proud! Take your place on the popular terraces of English Football Clubs, stand shoulder-to-shoulder bravely with your fellow fans. Urge on your favourites! Sing out! Sing up!

WE ARE THE CHAMPIONS!

...THE TRUE INTENT OF FOUL LANGUAGE IS THAT OF HONEST INSULT & PURE ABUSE.